PRAISE FOR *THE SACRED SLOW*

"This book is simply stunning. Whether you're exhausted by emptiness or worn thin from weariness, you'll discover healing, restoration, and the God-life waiting for you in these pages. That gut-level, gnawing sense that there's got to be more—well, it wasn't your imagination. This book will help you spelunk the depths of God like never before."

—MARGARET FEINBERG
AUTHOR OF *FLOURISH*

"In a world where the words *fast, instant, automatic, rapid, speedy, ready-made,* and *prefabricated* are marketed as that which is preferable and desirable, mistakenly there has developed a spirituality that trumpets the instantaneous, the quick, the immediate, and the right now as being signs of the hand of God. This has resulted in what Alicia Britt Chole correctly terms 'fast faith.' In *The Sacred Slow*, Alicia provides a corrective call away from addiction to experiences and into developing intimacy with God. With the care of a seasoned spiritual director, she lovingly takes us on a deliberate journey into points and places of transparency and closeness with God that can only occur over time. It is a journey well worth taking."

—BISHOP CLAUDE R. ALEXANDER JR.
SENIOR PASTOR, THE PARK CHURCH, CHARLOTTE, NC

"It's hard to find an appropriate sentence or two to describe *The Sacred Slow*. It's like asking someone to describe their life in three minutes—impossible! Alicia has poured thirty years and countless hours into this content, asking the reader to breathe, to think, to dig deep, to see soul health restored, and in turn, to see the joy of daily living reinstated. With my whole heart I endorse not only the book but the writer, who lives as she writes and walks as she asks us to. Take the time and dive in deep."

—DARLENE ZSCHECH
PASTOR, WORSHIP LEADER, AUTHOR

"We live speedy lives today—yet fast can quickly become an enemy of the good, and it's easy to miss God when you're rushing by. So how do we enter a life of wonder and fullness? How do we RSVP yes to God's invitation for listening and rest? Alicia Britt Chole is a trusted guide to help you live present to the God who is already present to you. In *The Sacred Slow*, she distills from her thirty-plus years of experience mentoring others to provide not only biblical concepts but practical tools for application that can help us enter God's sacred invitation to go deeper in life with him."

—JOSHUA RYAN BUTLER
PASTOR AT IMAGO DEI COMMUNITY (PORTLAND, OR); AUTHOR
OF *THE PURSUING GOD* AND *THE SKELETONS IN GOD'S CLOSET*

"*The Sacred Slow* is the fruit of a carefully crafted and vetted mentoring sequence that emphasizes that intimacy with God is intentional, not accidental. This spiritual guidebook stresses process over product and demonstrates that without *shabbat* there is no *shalom*. It wonderfully portrays the often-missing skills of listening, stillness, waiting, and attentiveness that are critical components of abiding in Jesus."

—KENNETH BOA
REFLECTIONS MINISTRIES, ATLANTA, GA

"There are two words that absolutely should never be placed together in the same sentence: *fast faith*. And in this deeply intimate and fulfilling book, Alicia does a superb job in explaining why! *The Sacred Slow* takes us on a journey straight into the presence of our heavenly Father and it leaves us there to learn, to grow and to experience Him as never before. Alicia is an excellent mentor, coach, and friend throughout this journey. This book is a must-read for any Christian who wants to understand the true secret to intimacy with God."

—JENNIFER KEITT
NATIONALLY SYNDICATED RADIO
HOST OF *THE JENNIFER KEITT SHOW*

"In *The Sacred Slow*, Alicia uses her stirring story to help us dare to look at our own. Her candor and truthfulness about her life's highs and lows have taken her to levels of depth and growth that few of us know even exists. As she sensitively bears her soul, we are caught up in making the whole of our lives a loving dialog with Jesus. She cuts and cures. As I read, I felt she was reading me—and in my faith journey *with* me. Alicia has accepted that pain is often a gift, so her story is transformational, without bringing attention to herself. I wouldn't have missed dwelling in this book!"

—GAIL MACDONALD
AUTHOR OF *HIGH CALL, HIGH PRIVILEGE*; SERVES
AS CHANCELLOR AND WIFE AT DENVER SEMINARY
ALONGSIDE HER HUSBAND, GORDON MACDONALD

"The title *The Sacred Slow* not only describes the content but also describes Alicia and her writing. Every now and then you come across a person whose presence and writing has a sense of the *sacred*. When you read Alicia's writing, you quickly know she is a person who has a deep, rich, winsome, and life-giving relationship with God. And, like enjoying an exquisite meal, it is best enjoyed *slow*. She is such a gifted writer that every sentence and paragraph must be slowly pondered and absorbed. This book is a wonderful blend of insight, inspiration, and invitation."

—LANCE WITT
FOUNDER, REPLENISH MINISTRIES

"Alicia is a trusted and gentle guide offering profound wisdom and thoughtfulness into a new way to live. Quietly and slowly taking time with these pages will change your life."

—NATHAN FOSTER
DIRECTOR OF COMMUNITY LIFE, RENOVARÉ;
AUTHOR OF *THE MAKING OF AN ORDINARY SAINT*

"Dr. Alicia Britt Chole practically explains how to reorient your life so that rather than living *for* God (or anything else) you learn to live *with* God—a subtle shift that offers life-giving fruit. Her road map is delivered in easily digested bits that encourage reflection, sustainability, and growth that is healthy for your mind, body, and soul. In an age full of cacophonous distraction, *The Sacred Slow* has the power to lead you on a spiritual journey that will truly change your life."

—DR. HOLLY CARLSON ZHAO
NEUROPSYCHOLOGIST; DIRECTOR OF THE CENTER
FOR OPTIMAL BRAIN HEALTH

THE
SACRED
SLOW

THE
SACRED
SLOW

A HOLY DEPARTURE FROM FAST FAITH

alicia britt chole

W PUBLISHING GROUP

AN IMPRINT OF THOMAS NELSON

Published in Nashville, Tennessee, by W Publishing, an imprint of Thomas Nelson.

Thomas Nelson titles may be purchased in bulk for educational, business, fund-raising, or sales promotional use. For information, please e-mail SpecialMarkets@ ThomasNelson.com.

Unless otherwise noted, Scripture quotations are taken from the Holy Bible, New International Version®, NIV®. Copyright © 1973, 1978, 1984, 2011 by Biblica, Inc.™ Used by permission of Zondervan. All rights reserved worldwide. www.zondervan. com. The "NIV" and "New International Version" are trademarks registered in the United States Patent and Trademark Office by Biblica, Inc.™

Scripture quotations marked KJV are from the King James Version. Public domain.

Scripture quotations marked THE MESSAGE are from *The Message*. Copyright © by Eugene H. Peterson 1993, 1994, 1995, 1996, 2000, 2001, 2002. Used by permission of NavPress. All rights reserved. Represented by Tyndale House Publishers, Inc.

Any Internet addresses, phone numbers, or company or product information printed in this book are offered as a resource and are not intended in any way to be or to imply an endorsement by Thomas Nelson, nor does Thomas Nelson vouch for the existence, content, or services of these sites, phone numbers, companies, or products beyond the life of this book.

ISBN 978-0-7180-9430-0 (TP)

ISBN 978-0-7180-9496-6 (eBook)

Library of Congress Cataloging-in-Publication Data

Library of Congress Control Number: 2017946408

Printed in the United States of America

24 25 26 27 28 LBC 13 12 11 10 9

Dedicated to my insightful and hilarious youngest, Louie.

When you were two, you pulled out a big blanket and
explained, "Mommy sicky. I tuck you." When all the
corners were tightly crumpled under my limbs, you
looked at your work with contentment and concluded,
"It's cold and the dogs are going poop."

This is a book about healing in the midst of real life.

When you were three, I took you and Keona to the voting station.
You brought your box of Band-Aids, and when I asked why, you
replied, "Because there may be people who are hurting here."

This is a book about the power of choice in a world filled with pain.

When you were four, you asked, "What is heaven?" "Heaven
is the place Jesus has prepared for those who believe in Him,"
I responded. "Oh, so that's where we become real again?"
you offered. "Yes, that's where we become real," I replied.

This is a book about becoming real.

When you were five, your teenage brother moaned, "Welcome
to *my* world." You corrected him immediately: "It's not your
world. It's God's world. You have to create it to own it."

*This is a book about honoring God as Creator
and ourselves as God's art.*

When you were almost six, the electricity suddenly went out
at a friend's home. The other children were alarmed. But you,
with perfect calm, said, "It's okay. The sun is still on."

*This is a book about how God is equally
present in the light and in the dark.*

When you were seven, you were making a case for why I should
let you do something, and your crowning argument was,
"But, Mom, I've been waiting to do this since tomorrow!"

*This is a book about time as a good gift and
waiting as a sacred discipline.*

When you were eight, you stood smiling at the snow,
deep in thought. Then you sighed and said, "That's what
I love about winter. You can see where the birds go."

This is a book about developing a habit of attentiveness in every season.

When you were nine, on the day I turned in this manuscript,
you asked, "Daddy, will you be alive when I retire?" Barry said,
"Well, that might be hard. I'll be well over one hundred." You
replied, "Oh, I guess I will have to chew your food for you."

Ultimately, this is a book about love.
And love is what you have taught me.

(I think you'll like this book.)

CONTENTS

MOVEMENT FIVE—CENTRALIZING HIS PRESENCE

MOVEMENT SIX—RELATING TO HIS WORD

MOVEMENT SEVEN—DISCOVERING GOD-PRINTS

MOVEMENT EIGHT—THE DISCIPLINE OF RESTRAINT

MOVEMENT NINE—A THEOLOGY OF TIME AND SPACE

Movement Ten—Unexpected Friends

Movement Eleven—Sabbath and Prayer Retreats

Movement Twelve—The Sacred Go

Toolbox

INTRODUCTION

In focus, *The Sacred Slow* is more like a marathon than a one-hundred-yard dash. The finish line will not be visible from the starting block.

In intensity, this holy departure from Fast Faith will feel more like a thru-hike than a morning workout. A high-energy start would be counterproductive.

In composition, these fifty-two experiences in unhurried honesty with God will build on and benefit deeply from every book, retreat, and Bible study you have known and still be *other*.

Perhaps it will help to understand my role in your reading. At our cores, my husband and I are both people-growers. Over the decades, some have referred to us as mentors, spiritual directors, or healthy-soul coaches. Whatever the label, our focus is prayerfully guiding learners and leaders into intentional and sustainable intimacy with God.

If you were to commit to fifty-two mentoring sessions with us, the essential content we would work through together is what you hold in your hands.

After twenty-five years of providing customized spiritual mentoring, I spent the twenty-sixth year designing *The Sacred Slow* and then the next five years field-testing its content. Every sentence you are about to read is rooted in three certainties:

1. Moment-by-moment nearness with God can be a reality for all sincere followers of Jesus regardless of personality or position in life.

2. Though such intimacy with God is attainable, it is not accidental. Sustained nearness is the cultivated fruit of intentionality.

3. Spiritual intentionality connects us with God and with what He sees, celebrates, and weeps over.

In other words, intimacy with God is not the exclusive domain of monks in monasteries or contemplatives in cloister. Right where you are, in moments both ordinary and extraordinary, you and Jesus can live attentive to each other. Whatever your work, it can be done in Jesus, with Jesus, and for Jesus. Nearness with God in no way dooms us to drown in the depths of introspection. On the contrary, it sensitizes us to the John 3:16 world that God so loved when He gave His only Son for our sins.

Those who have journeyed before you through this content share a similar story: they began reading something that ultimately read them.

There is nothing remotely passive about these pages. The readings, though conversational, are not random. The exercises, though diverse, are not disconnected. Together, each experience (I hesitate to call them chapters) will invite you into a fierce and freeing honesty about yourself, your faith, and your God.

But please know that honesty alone is not the end goal of the journey. Honesty is a means to cultivating deep and enduring love. Each unhurried, honest answer to every unhurried, honest question will work together to remove layers of misthink and overdo in our souls.

The twelve movements of *The Sacred Slow* are sequenced intentionally:

One—Two Stories
Two—Adding Intentionality

Within each movement, my responsibility is to provoke thought and press applications to mentor you in thinking anew about what God really wants from you.

Your responsibility is simply to be true. Honesty is the one thing you must bring to the table. So, read (prayerfully), respond (with as much uncensored honesty as you can offer), and anticipate the renewal that only God's love can bring.

> Honesty is a friend of intimacy with God and, conversely, denial is an enemy of intimacy with God. . . . Fast denial. Be honest with yourself so that you can be honest with your God.[1]

TWO STORIES

PATIENT TRUST

> Above all, trust in the slow work of God.
> We are quite naturally impatient in everything
>   to reach the end without delay.
> We should like to skip the intermediate stages. . . .
> And yet it is the law of all progress
>   that it is made by passing through
>   some stages of instability—
>   and that it may take a very long time. . . .
> Give Our Lord the benefit of believing
>   that his hand is leading you,
> and accept the anxiety of feeling yourself
>   in suspense and incomplete.[1]
>
> —PIERRE TEILHARD DE CHARDIN, S.J.
> *HEARTS ON FIRE: PRAYING WITH JESUITS*

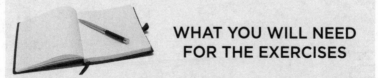

WHAT YOU WILL NEED FOR THE EXERCISES

✔ Life Scroll (in the Toolbox in the back of the book)
✔ A fine-point permanent marker

WHAT IS FAST FAITH?

Ours is a hurried age in which speed is deified and waiting is demonized.

Ours is a cluttered age in which noise is the norm and images constantly clamor for our attention.

And in our hurried, cluttered age, *faster* has become synonymous with *better*, and *experience* has become a substitute for *relationship*.

The problem, however, is that faster experiences do not produce better relationships with people or with God.

Relationship with God is best fed by a steady practice of attentiveness to God (as opposed to a diet of relative neglect, interrupted occasionally by quick spikes of engagement and intense surges of experience), which may help explain some of the spiritual dissatisfaction and burnout puzzling countless sincere souls in our day. We mistake the spikes and surges for spiritual strength and are left wondering why our faith at times still feels uneven and lonely.

Changing such age-old patterns requires new thinking, and that, at first, can seem strenuous. We are so attached to—and consequently so protective of—our fast, experiential, adrenaline-addicted culture that we confidently call physical spikes *energy* and spiritual spikes *inspiration*. And when the physical and spiritual align—when we feel something tangible in our senses while thinking something spiritual in our minds—we call it *intimacy with God*.

The potential combinations of surges and spikes are almost

endless in an age where many, but certainly not all, Jesus-followers suffer an embarrassment of spiritual riches. Inspirational quotes are at our fingertips. Moving devotionals remind us that God's mercies are new multiple times every morning. Books abound. The best of the best sermons, interviews, and teachings are instantly accessible. These ever-expanding options are then supercharged by prayerfully and carefully crafted weekly services and truly breathtaking seasonal conferences and conventions.

However, God did not architect us to live—physically or spiritually—on adrenaline surges, however excellent their choreography may be. By divine design, we flourish with a connectivity that is more even and steady: one that accompanies each breath and affects each step. Faith is a glorious opportunity to live *in Him*—with or without the experience of feelings—through willful, moment-by-moment attentiveness to Jesus, Whose presence neither surges nor wanes.

Fast Faith, in contrast, lives surge to surge, ever alert to formulas and combinations that help the feelings linger longer.

Fast Faith interprets the sensory crashes in between surges not as waning adrenaline or normalization but rather as a lack of devotion or—even more erroneously—as the absence of God.

Fast Faith is a restless spirituality that often craves what is *new* and what is *next*, in the recycled hope that the latest "it" can satisfy an ache that can only be described as timeless.

And sadly, Fast Faith is also one of the reasons a generation is departing from Christianity to explore other religions that promise inner peace. To date, I have never heard anyone excuse him- or herself from the table because there were not enough excellent or exciting offerings to choose from, but because, after eating, he or she still felt hungry. Their complaint is about sustainability: "It was great. But it just didn't last." So he or she keeps wandering in search of something that will endure, in search of a feeling that can *remain*.

In truth, only God *remains.*
And God is not a feeling.

(II) GUIDED RESPONSE

Before You Begin

Each of the fifty-two experiences in *The Sacred Slow* contains two components—a reading and a guided response. Every guided response offers two options for engagement through a thought focus or an exercise.

The thought foci are questions or statements for reflection, personal journaling, or conversation with friends. The exercises are strategic sets of action steps designed to mentor you in the holy habit of intentionality toward your spiritual formation. Some will feel fun and natural, and others may feel clumsy and uncomfortable. For this context, the latter are needed as much as the former.

How long it will take to experience *The Sacred Slow* depends on what is best for you.

Though diverse in style and length, the readings are relatively short and can be scanned in a day. A prayerful consideration of each chapter's reading and its thought focus might take one or two weeks. To meaningfully engage in the readings and the exercises, I recommend twelve weeks—which is why the book is formatted in twelve movements. However, many have taken an even slower pace and sat with one chapter a week for a year.

At the beginning of each new movement, consider your schedule and invest for the duration of that movement in *either* the thought focus or the exercise. You can always return and do the other level of response at another time.

Most often, both options will flow directly from the chapter reading. However, in the first two movements, the readings will focus on the story behind the book and the guided response options will focus on the story of your life.

For many, the first nine exercises are the most intense as far as requiring the cooperation of your head, heart, and hands. As a mentor, I would rather you choose the less intense level of response (the thought focus) if you think that the intensity of these first exercises might cause you to abandon *The Sacred Slow* prematurely.

Remember that consistency can still be creative. Maybe you will thrive reading *The Sacred Slow* at the same time every morning. Maybe you are wired more for an extended block of time to focus on the journey once a week. Either way, shape your experience to complement how God has designed you.

Thought Focus:

If your history were to be made into a movie, what sets would the director design as the backdrop for the most formative moments of your life?

Exercise:

1. Generate a list of three or four trusted souls who (a) know you very well and (b) are emotionally safe. These are individuals who love you enough to be honest and are healthy enough not to abuse you with that honesty.

2. Generate a list of three or four trusted souls whom you spiritually respect for the depth of their love for Jesus.

3. Contact each person listed with some version of the following: *I am working my way through a book with exercises that sometimes require input from respected friends. I'd like to ask if you'd pray for me whenever I come to mind and also if you would be willing to help me out by responding to a few questions along the way. I'd be honored if you can say yes, but there's no pressure and no problem if you need to say no.*

4. Begin creating your Life Scroll. The first five exercises of *The Sacred Slow* focus on the development of a timeline that will evolve into an insightful spiritual tool. As the rings of a tree trunk tell some of its story, your Life Scroll will enable you to see your life in layers and then interact with those layers anew in a way that is often healing.

   • Unfold your Life Scroll from the Toolbox in the back of the book. Make a timeline at the bottom edge of the page by labeling each tick with a year, starting with your birth and ending with next year.

   • Above the corresponding year, populate row 1 with information that the government and/or insurance companies have recorded, such as the date and city of your birth, significant dates in your family's history, out-of-country travel, dates and names of schools attended, when you received your driver's license, moves, jobs, new business endeavors, major purchases, illnesses, accidents, adoptions, etc.

   • For example, the first timeline tick at the base of my Life Scroll is labeled 1965. Above it, in the first row, I have written: *born in Las Vegas, NV.* Above 1990: *married Barry Jay Chole.* Above 1999: *son diagnosed with autism.* Above 2001: *Daddy died.* Above 2010: *purchased prayer retreat home.* Above 2013: *diagnosed with breast cancer.* Above 2016: *took daughter to Australia.* Above 2017: *published* The Sacred Slow.

With exercises like this, it is easy to spend the whole time mentally talking to yourself. Attempt to work through each part of this exercise conscious of God and in prayerful conversation with Him. He foresaw and was present for every single moment you are describing.

2

WHAT IS THE SACRED SLOW?

This God Who is not a feeling is the One Who established time. In the beginning, "there was evening, and there was morning—the first day" (Genesis 1:5). Time has not changed: it remains one of the few unaltered, original residents of the garden of Eden. Each day still holds roughly twenty-four hours, and each hour still holds approximately sixty minutes as Earth rotates on its axis in obedience to laws too old to be called ancient. Time, by divine design, is quite composed. Demand it to speed up or beg it to stand still, time will remain steady because it bows to only One. (And we, too, are His servants.)

However, each slow, calm tick of time has ceased to be a sacred reminder of the gift of life (let alone of the Giver of life). Now we view the steady, unhurried ticks as maddening reminders of what is undone. On the job, the undone may be a task. In our hearts, the undone is *us*.

> In reality, time is not the enemy.
> Faster is not the answer.
> Undone is not the problem.
> And slow is actually part of the solution.

Perhaps the real problem lies not with time but with our expectations. Since information travels at rates approaching the speed of light, we expect transformation to do the same. We want to grow faster and go faster and know faster than ever before. And if faith were a thing—a dead, inanimate thing—perhaps we could hurry it along by upgrading our technology.

Spiritual transformation, however, travels more at the speed of sound. To the point: we grow as we attend to the sound of God's love. If you just inadvertently rolled your eyes (or wondered how you could regift this book to some flowy friend), let me clarify. I have never heard that sound with my ears. Nor do I spend my days conjuring up the sound with my imagination. Attending to God's love is not the blissful fallout of sensationalism but the cultivated fruit of intentionality.

Welcome to the Sacred Slow.

The Sacred Slow is a holy departure from Fast Faith. It is a path that is both ancient (Enoch knew it) and holy (Jesus epitomized it).

Instead of going from surge to surge in pursuit of increasingly sticky spiritual experiences, the Sacred Slow invites you to willfully live in Him moment by moment by faith. Brother Lawrence described the contrast well:

> People seek for methods of learning to love God. They hope to arrive at it by I know not how many different practices. . . . Is it not much shorter and more direct to do everything for the love of God, to make use of all of the labors in one's state of life to show Him that love, and to maintain His presence within us by this communion of our hearts with His? There is no finesse about it; one has only to do it generously and simply.[1]

This "more direct" route is not remotely a denial of feelings or a dismissal of experiences. But it is a call to revoke the authority we have given our feelings to tell us whether or not God is in the room. Nor is this more direct route an elitist alternative reserved for certain personalities or professions. This way is open to all! As the sacred weight of slow living builds layer upon layer in our souls, we begin to live aglow from within, lit up in our minds and souls by increasingly continuous intimacy with God.

Be prepared; we will not begin by focusing on what Lawrence called "practicing the presence of God." We have some soul work to do to enable that adventure to become sustainable.

In the meantime, what should we do with our favorite experiences and practices? Enjoy them as you would any gift or privilege. The songs, books, teachings, and conferences are not the real problem. The real problem is our belief that these gifts are *how* or *where* we encounter God's presence.

God is not shyly hiding in the greenroom awaiting just the right atmosphere to make an appearance during a church service. Nor is He coyly withholding His presence from us until we play a certain song or open a specific book.

As you enter into the Sacred Slow, view these gifts not as sources of God's company but as celebrations of God's company. Delight in the gifts not as surges that usher in God's presence but rather as holy reminders that God is already, and always, with you. I am pretty sure that this is the deepest desire of the pastors who craft services, the worshipers who write songs, the authors who pen books, the preachers who record teachings, and the planners who painstakingly choreograph conferences.

They want you to know that the God you hear about and sometimes feel *there* is with you *everywhere*.

❚❚ GUIDED RESPONSE

Thought Focus:

Recall the three or four sets identified in chapter 1 of your life as a movie. Wrap words around what was happening within you spiritually in these formative sets or spaces.

Exercise:

1. God is with you! Conscious of that reality, open your Life Scroll in His presence and make one request: "God, walk with me through the years and show me, remind me, reveal to me significant moments in my journey with You."

2. In row 2 of your Life Scroll, write these pivotal, critical, landmark, or formative spiritual moments and experiences in the space above the corresponding year.

   • For example, in the space above my early childhood, I wrote: *attended mass with Mom.* Above 1974: *chose atheism as a belief system.* 1983: *God interrupted my atheistic existence.* 1994: *yearlong sabbatical.* 2013–2014: *thick experience of God's love during breast cancer surgery and recovery.*

   • Allow yourself to revisit these moments. Life Scroll memories may inspire prayer, gratitude, or tears. Give yourself permission to pause or ponder, worship or wonder, miss a loved one or write a letter to a dear one.

3. And then rest. Distancing ourselves from our story may (initially) appear easier. Being honest to our history can be hard work.

3

THE NUMBER OF REST

As you are prayerfully re-remembering your story through the guided responses, I will offer a glimpse into the story of this book. Very early in life, I came to the conclusion that God was man-made: an anxiety-inspired, artificial filler for gaps in knowledge. As a realist, I simply preferred unanswered questions to fairy tales. In high school, annoyingly optimistic Christian friends kept gifting me with tiny green Bibles. Much to their discouragement, the words in those Bibles seemed thinner to me than the paper on which they were printed.

But when Jesus interrupted my atheistic existence, the Bible was no longer a book: it was a Voice! By nature a student, hearing and studying that Voice has absolutely captivated me. Countless studies have delighted and strengthened my soul over the decades, one of which was an exhaustive study of the number seven (and all things "seventh") in the Bible.

A handful of numbers in the Scriptures have solid significance, and the number seven is surely one of them. Throughout the Scriptures, the number seven is associated with a counter-cultural slowing and a rigorous form of resting. Additionally, as you will soon discover, the number seven is of special importance to the Sacred Slow.

Consider the significance of the number seven in the Scriptures:

SEVEN
Literally, a prime number between six and eight
Figuratively, a symbol with spiritual weight

A seven-day test for Saul as Israel's king
Seven demons cast out of Mary Magdalene
Seven baskets of broken bread after the crowds ate
Seven years times two for Jacob to work and to wait
Seven powerless sons of Sceva humbled beyond words
Seven wise, Spirit-led men chosen by the church to serve
Seven dips in the Jordan River for the healing of Naaman
Seven rich years of plenty followed by seven years of famine
Seven final phrases of our Suffering Savior, Jesus Christ
Seven times for Elijah's servant to search the clear, blue skies
Seven days for work and for rest in the account of the creation
Seven churches forewarned and addressed in the book of
     Revelation
Seven days of marching in faith around the tall walls of
     old Jericho
A furnace seven-times hotter for Shadrach, Meshach, and
     Abednego[1]

Seven figures prominently in Scripture as a period of waiting, warring, warning, and wisdom. The number boundaries intentional times, set-apart spaces, moments kissed by the divine, and resting places.

In Genesis 2:2–3, God rested on the seventh day and called it holy. In Exodus 20:8–11, within the Ten Commandments, God called His people to set aside every seventh day as a holy day of rest. And in Leviticus 25:1–7, God gave His people instructions to set aside as sacred every seventh (Sabbath) year:

> The LORD said to Moses at Mount Sinai, "Speak to the Israelites and say to them: 'When you enter the land I am going to give you, the land itself must observe a sabbath to the LORD. For six years sow your fields, and for six years prune your vineyards and gather their crops. But in the seventh year the land is to have a year of

sabbath rest, a sabbath to the LORD. Do not sow your fields or prune your vineyards. Do not reap what grows of itself or harvest the grapes of your untended vines. The land is to have a year of rest. Whatever the land yields during the sabbath year will be food for you—for yourself, your male and female servants, and the hired worker and temporary resident who live among you, as well as for your livestock and the wild animals in your land. Whatever the land produces may be eaten.'"

Imagine being in the congregation on the day when Moses announced, "God is calling us to a Sacred Slow."

⏸ GUIDED RESPONSE

Thought Focus:

Movie trailers compress hours into minutes by featuring clips of high and low tension in the story. What "heights" would be in your life's trailer? Which "depths" could not be deleted in order for viewers to truly understand who you are today?

Exercise:

1. Cover (or ignore) row 2 of your Life Scroll so that you are only focusing on rows 1 and 3. Mentally page through your life story, making note of moments of genuine joy or celebration.

   - In row 3 of your Life Scroll, add these joyous moments above the corresponding year of your timeline.

   - For example, in row 3 of my Life Scroll, above 1987–1988, I have written: *lived in Singapore and Hong Kong and fell in love with Asia.* Above 2003: *Keona was born!!!* Above 2011: *launched nonprofit devoted to mentoring leaders—this is a convergence of all I love in ministry.*

2. Cover (or ignore) rows 2 and 3 of your Life Scroll so that you are only focusing on rows 1 and 4. Mentally page through your life story, making note of moments of genuine pain or sorrow.

   - In row 4 of your Life Scroll, add these bruising, disappointing, or painful moments above their year in the timeline. Unless you choose otherwise, you are the only one who will see your Life Scroll, so feel free to make these notes as detailed or as vague as you like.

   - For example, in row 4, above 1977, I noted: *the piano was my counselor during a two-year depression.* Above 1988: *a pastor had an affair with a friend—devastating for the entire ministry.* Above 2005: *three months of paralyzing pain from surgery reactions.*

As you walk through the addition of these two layers, remain alert to your emotions. Over what memories did you rush? Linger? Feel resistance? Experience joy? Struggle to describe? Want to dilute or embellish? Acknowledge (but do not try to explain) these responses in quiet conversation with God.

THE ORIGINAL SACRED SLOW

A commandment
From God
Through Moses
Given on Mount Sinai
One year removed from Egypt
En route to the promised land

As a title, *The Sacred Slow* takes its inspiration from one of the oldest and most forgotten commands of God. Immediately following instructions establishing a Sabbath day, the Passover, the Feast of Weeks, and the Day of Atonement, and immediately before instructions establishing the year of Jubilee, God called His people to observe every seventh year as a Sabbath year.[1]

Listed among the first recorded commands of God in Exodus and among the last recorded words of Moses in Deuteronomy, the Sabbath Year instructions emphasized four components:

1. freedom for Hebrew slaves[2] (Exodus 21:1–4; Deuteronomy 15:12–15;[3] Jeremiah 34:14),[4]
2. rest for the land (Exodus 23:10–11; Leviticus 25:1–7),[5]
3. cancellation of all Israelite debt[6] and generosity to those in need (Deuteronomy 15:1–18; 31:10),[7] and
4. hearing the Law as a community (Deuteronomy 31:9–13).[8]

Why? What might have been the purpose of a Sacred Slow in the lives of the first hearers?[9] Old Testament and Hebrew scholar Andrew Shead[10] identifies two premises in Leviticus 25 that undergird Sabbath Year and Jubilee legislations, both of which emphasize God as the Giver of land and soul.

> First, land cannot be owned because God already owns it (v. 23). Israel possessed it only by gift, their inheritance as members of a divine-human kinship system. . . . Secondly, because Israelites are God's slaves, they cannot be one another's slaves or sold as slaves to outsiders (vv. 42, 55).[11]

Moses' stated purpose seems to affirm Shead's conclusions: "Remember that you were slaves in Egypt and the LORD your God redeemed you. That is why I give you this command today" (Deuteronomy 15:15). In other words,

> As you free others, *remember* how God freed you.
> As you rest the land, *remember* who truly owns it.
> As you cancel debts, *remember* who cancelled yours.
> As you listen to the Law, *remember* the price your forefathers paid for not listening.

Whereas such remembrance would have sown humility, actual application would have sown trust. Hardship was embedded in the Sabbath Year experience, and the most challenging of hardships awaited the year's conclusion.[12]

Imagine.

> Corporate listening to the Law began the season.
> Workers did not work the land, and landowners did not profit from the land.

Those in financial crises were given a fresh start.
Indentured servants were set free.
The promised land rested.

Imagine.

Rest the land and hear the Law:
> Cease laboring and rediscover the substance of
> God's Word.

Release indentured servants and cancel debts:
> Purge from your life the careful counting of what
> others owe you.

Make no profit and give generously:
> Fast from accumulation and practice tangible love
> to those in need.

In an agricultural society, such a year would drastically change the fabric of a community. Space would be startling (and space is very telling).

But *only* imagine, because it appears that the community never heeded this original Sacred Slow until after their exile.

⏸ GUIDED RESPONSE

Self. In one sense, *self* is a curious and complicated concept: hard to define, close to impossible to draw, the subject of endless books, and the focus of famous philosophers.[13] In another sense, *self* is a familiar and simple concept: near, dear, and (most days) clear. This second sense is our current emphasis. There is no need to dust off old textbooks on Jungian psychology. For these guided response options, you only need space to think, honesty to see, and a wide array of adjectives.

Thought Focus:

Continuing with the movie analogy, imagine yourself as a casting director. How would you describe your character to a potential actor trying out for the role? What attributes and qualities would the actor need to be able to portray? The purpose of this thought focus is to give us insight into how we see ourselves historically.

Exercise:

1. Cover (or ignore) rows 2 through 4 so that you are only focusing on rows 1 and 5. Consider each season of your timeline in row 1, and ask, "How did I see myself in this space or season? What did I think of myself as a child, in high school, at that church, in that role, etc.?" (Though often related, please keep in mind that this is a different question from, "What did *others* think of me?")

2. In row 5 of your Life Scroll, list adjectives that capture these self-perceptions above the corresponding year in the timeline.

   - For example, I will need to take an educated guess for my early childhood. My mother refused to abort me even though the doctor told her she would probably die delivering me. Though few memories remain from my early years, I am pretty sure that I viewed myself as *celebrated* and *treasured*. Around the age of twelve, with acne and peer rejection in high gear, I saw myself as a *pimply, weirdly smart misfit*. When Jesus mercifully awakened me to His existence, I viewed myself as *the most fortunate college student on earth*.

   - As an adult, I was in a context where a leader regarded my strengths as weaknesses. In this space I can easily describe how I *felt* (confused, wounded, and—for the first time I am aware of—angry), but it takes a bit more work to move from how I felt to how I saw myself. For me, this part of my story needed a two-step process. First, I described how I felt: *confused* and *wounded*. Second, I stretched to realize how I viewed myself: *undone*, *lost*, and *small*.

Some descriptors will come quickly while others will take some waiting and praying. Silence is a good friend for such a process. If you feel stuck or sense that you may be overthinking the exercise, take a break, or combine your thinking with a physical activity like stretching, walking, hiking, or biking.

Though we are speaking of *self* in simple terms, this will not be a simple exercise. For some, this may be the most mentally and emotionally taxing layer to discern. Ask a friend to be praying for you while you work through row 5.

GOD'S ISSUE WITH CLENCHED FISTS

Picture the Israelite community gathered in a sacred assembly, listening intently to the contents of Leviticus for the first time:

> One day a year for the Day of Atonement.
> One day a week for the Sabbath.
> One week a year for Passover and for the Feast of Tabernacles.
> One year every seven devoted to rest in the promised land.

I wonder if one or two in the crowd thought, *Wait. Did Moses just say a year? A WHOLE YEAR? Then this is multiple choice, right? Surely God wouldn't ask me not to work AND to release those who work for me. Certainly He's too reasonable to ask me not to make a profit AND to give generously with no income in sight.*

Reasonable?

Reasonable is in the eye of the beholder.

But God does seem to consistently take issue with clenched fists.

In the beginning, we open our eyes and instinctively tighten our grip around all that is placed in our hands. In the end, others close our eyes, and our hands are incapable of gripping a single thing.

Perhaps on the other side we may see this life as a journey from keeping to releasing, from gripping to entrusting.

A clenched fist displays the delusion of ownership.
An open hand reveals the realities of stewardship.

The original Sacred Slow was a corporate exercise in refreshing an open-handed existence. Stuff is sticky. Releasing is a form of deliverance. In His wisdom, God crafted a space for His people to delight in the discipline of dependence.

And for possibly 490 years, it appears that the community shunned the space, ignored the command, and eventually raised their clenched fists in rebellion toward God.

The spiritual formation potential of the Sabbath Year was rich indeed. However, such wealth seems to have been unrealized until after the Israelites' exile. Immediately after the command was initially given in Leviticus 25, God clearly identified two consequences for disobedience in Leviticus 26: exile for His people and rest for the land.

If in spite of this you still do not listen to me but continue to be hostile toward me . . . Your land will be laid waste, and your cities will lie in ruins. Then the land will enjoy its sabbath years all the time that it lies desolate and you are in the country of your enemies; then the land will rest and enjoy its sabbaths. All the time that it lies desolate, the land will have the rest it did not have during the sabbaths you lived in it. (vv. 27, 33–35)

True to His word,

He carried into exile to Babylon the remnant, who escaped from the sword, and they became servants to him and his successors until the kingdom of Persia came to power. The land enjoyed its sabbath rests; all the time of its desolation it rested, until the seventy years were completed in fulfillment of the word of the LORD spoken by Jeremiah. (2 Chronicles 36:20–21)[1]

We see further evidence of the Israelites' understanding that their exile was in part connected to ignoring the Sabbath Years when Nehemiah came to Jerusalem to rebuild the wall around 445 BC. Upon its completion, the community made a binding agreement with God. Among their commitments, they stated, "Every seventh year we will forgo working the land and will cancel all debts" (Nehemiah 10:31).

Though the promise was reinstituted, significant debate exists over the "when" (and even the "if") of Sabbath Year application by God's people.[2] Scholars do agree, however, that during the Israelites' exile, the generation that originally heard the Sabbath Year command passed away while the promised land rested. The spiritual formation potential of the command would await discovery by subsequent generations.

What could have been avoided—let alone gained—if the community had embraced the space?

⏸ GUIDED RESPONSE

Thought Focus:

Recall the key spaces you have identified in your life as a movie so far: formative sets, critical spiritual influences, a trailer with clips of heights and depths, qualities of the lead actor who would play your part. Now ask a weighty question: Where is God in each scene?

Exercise:

1. Cover (or ignore) rows 2 through 5 so that you are only focusing on rows 1 and 6. Consider each season of your timeline and think about your perceptions of God.

2. In row 6, list your God-perceptions above the corresponding year of the timeline in response to this prompt: *In this space/season/time, I saw God as* _____.

   - For example, as a young atheist, above 1975–1983, I wrote: *nonexistent, fear-inspired fiction.* Above 1983, after the God encounter: *Pursuer. Forgiver.* Above 2000: *Mysterious. Dream-giver and dream-killer. Untamable.* Above 2015: *Warrior. Extravagant Father.*

   - Over some years you may want to write: *Inconsistent. Distant. Silent.* Be brutally honest with yourself and with God. For His part, God is rather secure. Resist the urge to tidy up your gut-level God-concepts. Even when it is messy, honesty is still a friend of intimacy with God.

ADDING INTENTIONALITY

" The amount of responsibility one takes for his or her
own life is the quintessential issue of leadership and self.[1]
—EDWIN H. FRIEDMAN, *A FAILURE OF NERVE*

WHAT YOU WILL NEED
FOR THE EXERCISES

✔ Your Personal Inventory (in the Toolbox in the back
of the book)
✔ A few wise friends

THE UNDERESTIMATED DANGER OF NOT LISTENING

Jeremiah 29:11–13 is one of the most quoted verses in all of Scripture:

> "For I know the plans I have for you," declares the LORD, "plans to prosper you and not to harm you, plans to give you hope and a future. Then you will call on me and come and pray to me, and I will listen to you. You will seek me and find me when you seek me with all your heart."

Jeremiah 29:10 is not:

> This is what the LORD says: "When seventy years are completed for Babylon, I will come to you and fulfill my good promise to bring you back to this place."

When seventy years are completed: one year for every Sabbath Year God's people refused to embrace.

> "But *you did not listen to me*," declares the LORD, "and *you have aroused my anger with what your hands have made*, and you have brought harm to yourselves."

Therefore the LORD Almighty says this: "Because *you have not listened to my words* . . . This whole country will become a desolate wasteland, and these nations will serve the king of Babylon seventy years." (Jeremiah 25:7–8, 11, emphasis mine)

How hard it is to anticipate the full reach of willful sin. Who among the people could have guessed that not listening would lead to idolatry?[1] *Not listening* seems so small, almost benign, and easily justified as a temporary postponement of obedience.

Yet, not listening is perhaps the first exhale of lovelessness.

Listening is a posture of attentiveness, which acknowledges the presence of another.

Listening is an exercise in interdependence, which nurtures a teachable spirit.

Not listening is not.

Not listening is a posture of arrogance, which ignores the contributions of another.

Not listening is an exercise in independence, which breeds a rebellious spirit.

By not listening, God's people "brought harm to [them]selves" (Jeremiah 25:7).

Which returns us to the ancient and forfeited power of the Sabbath Year—of space squandered, of listening denied.

Which returns us to the current and immeasurable potential of the Sacred Slow—of space devoted, of listening cherished.

Much has changed since Moses first announced the original Sacred Slow. Slavery is now illegal, few completely live off the land, most debts are held by banks, not by brothers, and we can hear God's Word by pushing a button, not only on communal feast days.

Two things have not changed. We still struggle to listen and obey, and not listening is still toxic for our souls and communities.

Today, we are in dire need of sacred and slow seasons to physically, figuratively, and emotionally release those who are bound, rest land, cancel debts, and hear God's Word in community. As Marjorie J. Thompson stated, "In a world driven by the need to accomplish and acquire, in a world where we judge one another on the basis of performance, God calls us to the radical trust of rest."[2]

On this side of the empty tomb, we have the privilege of discovering what Jesus called "rest for your souls" (Matthew 11:29) at depths and dimensions our ancestors in the faith ached to realize. In Jesus, soul-rest is entered through the cross[3] as Jesus' life, death, and resurrection release us from slavery to sin and free us from the vanity of works-based righteousness.

With and in Jesus, we then guard and grow that rest willfully through accepting forgiveness and rejecting the self-punishment of shame, stewarding our bodies and creation as God's art, forgiving and giving to others as Jesus has forgiven and given to us, and respecting God's Word personally and living it out in community.

This Sacred Slow is an ongoing invitation to truly listen.

This Sacred Slow is an ongoing exercise in an open-handed existence.

⏸ GUIDED RESPONSE

Thought Focus:

Reflect on your life as a movie, and write a review from two perspectives: your own and God's. Be honest about how your review may differ from His.

Exercise:

In Movement One, you created a Life Scroll with different layers of your story. In Movement Two, you will intentionally mix these layers (to reveal more than can be seen when they are considered in isolation) and then invite the past to help you live deliberately in the present. History is a willing teacher. She merely requires pupils committed to listening.

1. Quiet your heart before God. Ask the Holy Spirit to guide and teach you through the past as you personalize Psalm 139:1–4:

   > You have searched me, LORD,
   >> and you know me.
   > You know when I sit and when I rise;
   >> you perceive my thoughts from afar.
   > You discern my going out and my lying down;
   >> you are familiar with all my ways.
   > Before a word is on my tongue
   >> you, LORD, know it completely.

2. Unfold your Life Scroll and prayerfully mix various layers such as 1, 4, and 5; 1, 3, and 6; 1, 5, and 6. Then, in row 7, note any insights, connections, themes, or concerns that emerge. If helpful, use the following questions:
   - When these layers are viewed in relationship to one another, what do you see?
   - Are there any discoveries you want to explore further?
   - Does any part of your story seem clearer? Muddier?
   - What observations can you make regarding your development spiritually? Relationally? Professionally?

- Are there any connections between roots and fruits in your story that you would like to share with a friend or counselor?
3. In preparation for the next chapter's exercise, think about what you might hope to write in rows 5 and 6 in the coming years.

As I have mentioned before (and will mention again), resist the urge to self-guide in this exercise. Do this *with* Jesus. You are not alone. You have never been alone.

A CURIOUS REMEDY
FOR IDOLATRY

Not listening → *Idolatry* → *Exile*

Startling. Yet this is the flow of events revealed in the book of Jeremiah.

> Listening evidently strengthens a soul not to bow
> down to idols.
> Listening safeguards a heart against spiritual adultery.

No wonder the world is filled with such noise.

In Jeremiah 25, within a span of seven sentences, the community of faith was rebuked four times for their refusal to listen—twice by Jeremiah and twice by God.

> For twenty-three years—from the thirteenth year of Josiah son of Amon king of Judah until this very day—the word of the LORD has come to me and I have spoken to you again and again, but you have *not listened*.
>
> And though the LORD has sent all his servants the prophets to you again and again, you have *not listened* or paid any attention. (vv. 3–4, emphasis mine)

"But you *did not listen* to me," declares the LORD, "and you have aroused my anger with what your hands have made, and you have brought harm to yourselves."

Therefore the LORD Almighty says this: "Because you *have not listened* to my words . . ." (vv. 7–8, emphasis mine)

Each occurrence of *listen* in these passages is translated from the Hebrew עָמַשׁ (šā·mă'), which appears 1,161 times in Scripture, most often as *hear, hears,* and *heard.* This word, however, refers more to soul patterns than sound waves.

šā·mă' speaks of undivided attention and applied understanding.

šā·mă' is a spiritual discipline.

I find it weighty that immediately following this concentration of šā·mă' the Lord speaks of the silencing of favorite sounds:

Because you have not listened to my words . . . I will banish from them the sounds of joy and gladness, the voices of bride and bridegroom, the sound of millstones and the light of the lamp. (vv. 8, 10)

In the promised land, God's people—free and flourishing—practiced selective listening. They were attentive to celebratory sounds, but they ignored God's voice. They relished the sounds of feasting and commerce, but they tuned out voices of wisdom and conviction.

As Nebuchadnezzar conquered the nation, an unnatural silence covered Canaan. For seventy years, the land and God's people experienced an involuntary fast of their favorite sounds.

Though a logical consequence for refusing to listen, the silencing of celebratory sounds initially seems a curious remedy for purging a people of idolatry. We tend to want God to demonstrate His supremacy—and thereby squash our idolatry—through addition, not subtraction; through amplification, not through silence.

But silence is a purging force. Following the Exile, God's people never again wandered collectively into idolatry.

Through the story of the original Sacred Slow, it becomes clear that this discipline of šā·mă' can be cultivated in seasons of fullness. The people of God were repeatedly exposed to God's words and warnings in the promised land. But when we as God's people refuse to listen, He may gift us with involuntary fasts to remove pleasant distractions from our lives.

Exile enhances the senses.

Pain increases our overall sensitivity and grants us the opportunity to hear smaller sounds, like our own heartbeats and the soft splashes of God's tears.

⏸ GUIDED RESPONSE

Throughout the last six chapters of guided responses, we have prayerfully and strategically reflected on what has been. Now we turn our attention to partnering with God in what will be.

Time is a gift. Each day is full of potential. If we are alive, *experiencing* our futures is a given, but *realizing* our futures is not. The former only requires breath. The latter requires willful cooperation.

The difference between reactive existing and proactive participation is *intentionality*. The thought foci and exercises in chapters 7, 8, and 9 are designed to mentor us in willful spiritual intentionality.

Thought Focus:
Businesses spend sizable budgets to develop vision statements that give meaning to activity and momentum to dreams. Ask God to be

your life coach. Together, develop or refine a vision or purpose statement for this season of your life.

Exercise:

1. Consider the components of your Personal Inventory (PI) template in the Toolbox in the back of the book.[1] For a few minutes, think about the next three months of your life. Then commit the future to God through the following prayer:

   Great Shepherd of my soul, You have attended with care and love to every moment of my life. As I consider years past, I see Your hand clearly in some spaces. In other spaces, I acknowledge the presence of Your hand by faith, not by sight.

   Great Shepherd, You have gifted me with time and breath. In the coming days, I desire to partner with Your divine intentions for my life. Reveal to me how You long to grow me from this moment forward.

   Open my spiritual eyes to realize how You are mentoring me. I acknowledge that it requires little self-discipline to rush passionately toward the future. Strengthen me to slow down and walk in purposeful partnership with You into tomorrow and the days beyond, be they many or few.

2. Hold three questions prayerfully before God: What is Your heart for me in this season? What is Your focus as my Master Mentor? What emphasis would please You?

3. Then wait, write down anything that comes to mind, and string those thoughts together into a *season theme* for the next three months.
   - For example, themes for me over the years have included, "Live lean and love lavishly," "Invest deeper in fewer," "Prepare within for a new day of influence," and, "Rest—body, mind, and spirit."

- What if nothing comes to mind? That is okay. Listening has benefits whether or not anything is heard because it disciplines our minds. Look back at your response to chapter 6, exercise question 2, and draft a theme that reflects those desires.

The strength of a Personal Inventory is that it approaches the future heaven-down instead of only earth-up. In other words, we start with prayer (instead of planning) and listening (instead of lists).

Most self-improvement goals and New Year's resolutions start earth-up with what our eyes can see, what our hearts are worried about, or what annoys us. In contrast, PI's begin heaven-down with what God sees, what His heart longs for, and what would please Him. Earth-up lists are often about increasing productivity and decreasing failure. Heaven-down listening is about deepening relationship.

THE SOUND OF LISTENING

What then does it mean to truly listen?
Does it require the sense of hearing?

Consider master percussionist Evelyn Glennie, whose life mission is teaching people to listen. She is brilliant, skilled, and, since the age of twelve, profoundly deaf.

What does it mean to truly listen?
What are you listening to right now?

On one level, here in my favorite writing space, I am listening to audible sounds: the roll of thunder drawing near, leaves rustling wildly, and an occasional creak from a branch resting on the rooftop.

On another level, through waiting and writing, I am listening for something a microphone could not capture: the influence of God. How encouraging for happily common souls like mine that listening for the voice of God is not an elitist luxury reserved for those with multiple advanced degrees or perfect pitch or acclaimed lives or the ability to physically hear.

Since God breathed into us "the breath of life" (Genesis 2:7), our divinely touched dust has been honored with a standing invitation to listen for our Creator.

God's sound bookends the human story on earth from the first chapter of Genesis to the last chapter of Revelation.

And God said, "Let there be light," and there was light. (Genesis 1:3)

I, Jesus, have sent my angel to give you this testimony for the churches. I am the Root and the Offspring of David, and the bright Morning Star. . . .
    Yes, I am coming soon. (Revelation 22:16, 20)

The Genesis narrative introduces God's voice not at the creation of our "formless and empty" (Genesis 1:2) planet but at the installation of light. Before the first "Let there be," there was earth, water, and God's Spirit hovering over all. The Voice brought light—a light that preceded the creation of the sun.

The Revelation prophecy concludes with God's voice still bringing light. Over all the end-times images and earthly uncertainties rests the clear voice of the bright Morning Star as He assures listeners of His authority and His soon return.

A sound creates sound waves as it travels through air. In the same way, it seems that God's voice creates light waves whenever it is released. In the beginning of Genesis, light was visible. In the end of Revelation, the Light Himself was audible.

I ache to hear the Voice and see the Light in between.

Since God spoke in the beginning and speaks in the end, some have wondered if God is always speaking. Perhaps. Or—since God's voice is living—it could also be that everything He has spoken continues to sound throughout time.

Personally, I have never heard God's voice with my dust-formed ears. But listening in silence with the Scriptures, I sense the light waves of God's voice washing over my spirit and filling my mind.

Whether or not God is always speaking, I am unsure. But of this I am more certain: we *can* slowly and steadily develop the discipline of always listening.

The glorious mystery is that listening for God holds power whether or not anything is heard.

This clarion theme of spiritual listening stretches across the intertestamental period and continues to sound throughout the teachings of Jesus. Jesus talked a lot about listening.

> Whoever has ears, let them hear.[1]
> Whoever has ears to hear, let them hear.[2]
> Whoever has ears, let them hear what the Spirit says to
> the churches.[3]

Clearly, this is a challenge encountered by every generation of God-followers.

Clearly, physical "equipment" is not the issue.

In the Gospels and the book of Revelation, Jesus addressed a subject as old as, well, sin. Even surrounded by paradise on earth, humankind chose not to listen.

> You are free to eat from any tree in the garden; but you must not
> eat from the tree of the knowledge of good and evil, for when you
> eat from it you will certainly die. (Genesis 2:16–17)

No parables. No hidden meanings. Not even a riddle.

Such was the unambiguous voice of God to Adam, who evidently passed the instructions along to Eve.

Then Satan spoke the infamous, "Did God really say . . . ?" and with one well-placed interrogative, the deceiver called into question Eve's ability to hear precisely, remember accurately, and comprehend correctly. What was true then is still true today. The Enemy's tactics are especially effective when we, like Eve, are standing close enough to forbidden fruit for Satan to use it as a speaking prop.

Adam and Eve had heard God's audible voice. However, hearing has never been a synonym for heeding.

> "If anyone has ears to hear, let him hear.
>
>   "Consider carefully what you hear," he continued. "With the measure you use, it will be measured to you—and even more. Whoever has will be given more; whoever does not have, even what they have will be taken from them." (Mark 4:23–25)

We often quote this sowing and reaping principle from Jesus' teachings. However, wisdom invites us to remember that the context of Jesus' words was listening (not giving) and obeying (not proclaiming).

Hear.
  Consider carefully.
    The measure you use will be used for you.

Take notice.
  Observe and apply.
    The effort you exert will be reflected back to you by God.

⏸ GUIDED RESPONSE

Thought Focus:

A long time ago, I heard a concise response to the often pondered "Why do I exist?" from a missiologist named Steve Hawthorne: "To worship God and gather more worshipers for God."[4] Consider the relationship between the spiritual vision statement you identified in the last chapter and this eternal purpose shared by all who follow Jesus.

Exercise:

Throughout the crafting of your PI, keep in mind that this is a creative exercise. Think *with* God! Adjust the language at will to free yourself from any performance pressure. This tool is neither a measuring stick nor a taskmaster. It is the fruit of applied listening. In other words, the experiment is all win. By inclining your spiritual ears to proactively partner with God in your development, you have already added intentionality to your journey. And intentionality is a growth catalyst.

1. Turn to your PI and write down the season theme you worked on in the last chapter. Then identify areas of application that together provide coverage for your life. For example:
   - Season theme: Rest—body, mind, and spirit
   - Areas of application:
     (1) Physical
     (2) Family
     (3) Professional
     (4) Academic
     (5) Financial
     (6) Friendship
     (7) Other

2. Think with God (as opposed to brainstorming solo) about specific applications of your season theme. In each area ask, *God, how would You like me to apply this heaven-down theme in my daily life physically? Relationally? With work? At home?* Then write down applications that make sense and align with the theme. For example:
   - Season theme: Rest—body, mind, and spirit

- Areas of application:
  (1) Physical
    ◉ Each morning remind myself that I am God's art by placing Ephesians 2:10 on the mirror.
    ◉ Go offline at least an hour before bed and listen to classical music.
    ◉ Aim for eight hours of sleep nightly and fall asleep with a simple phrase like, "I love You, Lord" instead of worrying about tomorrow's to-do list.
  (5) Financial
    ◉ Switch to a cash system for snack breaks to decrease end-of-month bill stress.
    ◉ Go through my closet and give away a few good things to remind myself that I already have more than I need.
    ◉ Fast from purchasing anything beyond basic necessities for a month.
3. If nothing comes to mind for a specific area, go on to the next one. The goal is not to fill in blanks but to listen for God's desires. Continue the pattern of asking, listening, waiting, and writing until you have invested prayer in each potential area of application.

Throughout the process, resist thinking to yourself. Actively press your mind to stay in conversation with God. He has guided you through the awareness of a broad theme. He can inspire the details too. This is an exercise in listening prayer (not self-improvement) and intentional cooperation (not self-direction). Remember: God longs to mentor you.

[9]

SEED #3 AND THE ENEMY'S PLAN B

In Mark 4:34, we read that Jesus "did not say anything to them [the crowds] without using a parable. But when he was alone with his own disciples, he explained everything."

Everything.

(Wow.)

But of the "everything" Jesus explained—of all the parable interpretations Jesus provided His disciples—only two were included in the Gospels: Jesus' explanations of the parable of the sower and the parable of the weeds.

Both parables are underscored by Jesus' clarion call to hear and heed, which we have been considering. But the parable of the sower is further set apart by its appearance in all three Synoptic Gospels as well as by a riveting question from Jesus: "Don't you understand this parable? How then will you understand any parable?" (Mark 4:13).

Reading this question with a two-thousand-year-ish delay, uncertainty exists as to whether Jesus' disciples heard Him saying, "This parable is the *simplest to understand* of all parables" or, "This parable is *critical to understanding* all parables." Whether fundamental or foundational, the imagery is captivating, and I have returned to the parable of the sower repeatedly.

At first, the gardening images intrigued me. Through them, my spirit began to comprehend what my mind will never be able to formularize: the mysterious marriage of divine sovereignty and human responsibility, of God's initiation and our participation. Then I began studying the parable as a crescendo in God's cover-to-cover lament over how refusing to listen leaves His people vulnerable to deception and, ultimately, idolatry.

Somewhere along the way, a discovery surprised me. For perhaps the first decade of study, I assumed that only the seed in the fourth scenario—that fell upon good soil—survived and that the other three seeds—that fell on the path, on rocky places, and among thorns—perished.[1] Untrue. The seed in the third scenario also endured.

Two of the four seeds lived. The third survived constricted by thorns, and the fourth survived free to multiply. Jesus explained that,

> The seed falling among the thorns refers to someone who hears the word, but the worries of this life and the deceitfulness of wealth choke the word, making it unfruitful. But the seed falling on good soil refers to someone who hears the word and understands it. This is the one who produces a crop, yielding a hundred, sixty or thirty times what was sown. (Matthew 13:22–23)

> The seed that fell among thorns stands for those who hear, but as they go on their way they are choked by life's worries, riches and pleasures, and they do not mature. But the seed on good soil stands for those with a noble and good heart, who hear the word, retain it, and by persevering produce a crop. (Luke 8:14–15)

All of which causes me to wonder about the Enemy's plan B.

Sometimes we assume that if Satan cannot succeed in plan A (dragging our souls to hell[2] with him), then plan B must be inflicting our bodies with pain, exhausting our minds with worry, crushing our potential with ambition, or obsessing our souls with addictions.

Perhaps not.

Perhaps thorns such as the worries of this life, the deceitfulness of wealth, and the desires for other things are the means to the Enemy's ends, not ends in and of themselves. The Gospels state that the thorns were the means to a specific end: choking the Word to hinder it from maturing and, thereby, making it unfruitful.[3]

It seems that from Satan's perspective, the next best thing to spiritual death is spiritual barrenness.

In other words, if Satan cannot succeed in his plan A of taking your soul to hell with him, then plan B is to ensure that you do not take anyone else's soul to heaven[4] with you.

"Steal them or sterilize them" might be the kingdom of darkness's brutally efficient mission statement.

What distinguished the third barren seed from the fourth fruitful seed was intentionality. The fourth seed is described as a soul that, beyond hearing the Word, chose to *accept* the Word, *retain* the Word, *persevere* in the Word, and *produce* a crop through the Word.

This reality substantially broadens the scope of what is at stake when we refuse to hear and heed.

Our souls? Yes, and more.
We will live, but not multiply.

And by doing so, we will spend our days fulfilling Satan's plan B.

Thorns or fruit?
Evidently, the choice is ours.

❚❚ GUIDED RESPONSE

Thought Focus:

Our passivity is the Enemy's playground. Over the last two chapters, we have invested time in a spiritual vision statement. As we conclude this second movement, identify two realistic action steps you can take over the next month to add a fresh dimension of intentionality to the fulfillment of your God-given purpose.

Exercise:

1. Share your thoughtful, but not perfectly polished, PI with a few close, wise friends. Actively listen to their responses to some version/variation of the following:

   - What are your overall impressions as you read my Personal Inventory?
   - In your own words, what is the broad theme that God is speaking over my life?
   - Do any of the specific applications in any area appear unclear or unrealistic?
   - Is there anything I have expressed concern over that is not represented in my inventory? (Note that a "yes" is an invitation to pray, not a requirement to add it to your inventory.)

2. Adjust, edit, or clarify your PI in response to your friends' wisdom. Then place your PI before the Lord and commit your thoughts and plans to Him.

Resist all urges to plaster your refrigerator with Post-it note reminders or to recite your area applications before bedtime. Relax. God has a pretty remarkable memory. Our growth is better watered by meditating on who He is than by obsessing over who we are not. Occasionally, refer to your inventory as a means of recalling how God is leading you. Personally, I scan my PI for a few minutes during my monthly prayer retreats.

[Movement Three]

GOD-CONCEPTS

> " Were we able to extract from any man a complete answer
> to the question, "What comes into your mind when you
> think about God?" we might predict with certainty
> the spiritual future of that man. Were we able to know
> exactly what our most influential religious leaders think
> of God today, we might be able with some precision to
> foretell where the Church will stand tomorrow.[1]
>
> —A. W. TOZER, *THE KNOWLEDGE OF THE HOLY*

WHAT YOU WILL NEED FOR THE EXERCISES

✔ A notepad *or* journal
✔ Paper and pen *or* a computer
✔ Three painting canvases *or* sheets of white cardstock
✔ Paint *or* markers
✔ A timer
✔ A few good and honest friends

THE SOURCE OF
SPIRITUAL MISTHINK

We began *The Sacred Slow* by mapping our journeys to date and taking steps toward greater spiritual intentionality. This chapter marks our entrance into a weighty, critical space together.

When someone I am mentoring hits a wall of despair, despondency, or deception, the root issue is almost always some manifestation of misthink in the area of God-concept.

Spiritual misthink intimidates intimacy, cripples contentment, and deadens delight. Misthink distorts God's character to the Enemy's advantage and leaves a soul dangerously vulnerable to spiritual adultery.

Consider A. W. Tozer's perspective from *The Knowledge of the Holy*:

The essence of idolatry is the entertainment of thoughts about God that are unworthy of Him.[1]

The heaviest obligation lying upon the Christian Church today is to purify and elevate her concept of God until it is once more worthy of Him—and of her.[2]

The man who comes to a right belief about God is relieved of ten thousand temporal problems, for he sees at once that these have

to do with matters which at the most cannot concern him for very
long.[3]

Essence of idolatry. Heaviest obligation. Right belief. These are
carefully chosen words from a discerning pen. Yet how much energy
do we actually invest in identifying, purifying, and enriching our
God-concepts?

Perhaps precious little in comparison with our investment in
areas like leadership, relationships, future trends, current needs,
vision-casting, and ceiling-blasting.

Why?

Could it be that we have

- Thought that God-concepts were God's job?
- Believed that God-concepts were automatically downloaded
  as part of the salvation package?
- Assumed that God-concepts were naturally absorbed as we
  sat in church or opened a Bible?
- Checked "God-concept" off our list after that foundations
  Bible study series?
- Sincerely never thought about it?

My hope over the next few chapters is that any unseen negli-
gence would be banished by newfound vigilance. We live in a fallen
world. Sin seeds are indigenous to our humanity. The kingdom of
darkness constantly bombards us with impure and untrue messages
about life, faith, spirituality, and God.

The Word heard is not enough. It must be heeded.

Returning to the parable of the sower, what distinguished the
fourth soul was that beyond hearing, it *accepted* the Word (Mark
4:20). *Accept* is translated from *paradechomai*, which means "to
receive; to embrace with assent and obedience."[4]

Though the Word undeniably holds power, accurate God-concepts—that produce sustainable fruitfulness—are not formed by hearing the Word alone, but rather by embracing, assenting to, and obeying the Word.

We *quote* the Word over our weaknesses, worries, and wounds. We *proclaim* the Word over our dreams, families, and futures. May we now with intentionality *apply* the Word to the portrait we have painted of God.

⏸ GUIDED RESPONSE

This movement utilizes a variety of methods to help us identify and evaluate our working God-concepts. First, we will create a God-portrait with words or pictures.

Thought Focus:

Pay attention to your raw, unedited answers to this prompt at different times throughout your day: *God, right now I think You are* _____. If your response is less than flattering, do not worry about offending God. He already knows. Honesty gets us all on the same page.

Exercise:

1. On canvas or cardstock, create your first God-portrait by writing down the initial rush of adjectives and descriptions that come to mind in response to this prompt: *God, I honestly think You are* _____.

2. Fill the page with your responses as plainly or complexly as your artistic inclinations and time permit. This can be as concrete as written words penned on your canvas or as abstract as a collage of images from magazines or newspapers.

Freely include seemingly contradictory responses such as *loving* and *distant*, or *forgiving* and *stingy*. We are finite humans attempting to be honest about an infinite God. It is okay if our portraits are less than logical.

HOW TO WATER THORNS

Watering thorns.
Who would do such a thing?
Me.

"Those are pretty," I offered, as my husband and I walked hand in hand through the gently rolling land that surrounded our new home in Missouri.

"Yeeees," Barry said slowly, "but look at those thorns."

Knowing my aversion to cutting down indigenous trees, my husband smiled cautiously and warned, "We need to keep an eye on this."

A few years later, Arbor Dude (I am sure he had an official "ist" title, but I never could remember it) came to visit our sick 125-year-old oak tree and pointed toward the clump of thorn trees: "You have small children. I'd get rid of those if I were you."

The thorn trees under discussion are officially named honey locusts (an odd pairing of words from my perspective since I rarely place *honey* and *locust* in proximity). In tree-speak, *locust* is used to describe a variety of pod-carrying trees. The plague connection, however, is not entirely lost in this particular instance. One frustrated farmer called the honey locust, "the devil tree . . . that makes a cactus look cuddly."[1]

Though their fall foliage is beautiful and their pods contain a sweet pulp, honey locusts are aggressively invasive. They spread rapidly and are highly resilient to eradication. Their thorns can grow up to a foot in length and cause severe, infected, painful wounds in anyone unfortunate enough to come in contact with them.

We now have honey locust trees sprouting up throughout our property. Barry wrestles with them annually, and the kids, thankfully, know to steer clear of them. But it is sobering to realize that I contributed to the infestation.

I nurtured the thorn trees by omission. When I first saw them, I decided to do nothing. And doing nothing is a choice.

Watering thorns.
Who would do such a thing?
Us.

When we allow misthink to go unchecked, our choice to do nothing waters thorns. When we give ourselves permission to emotionally invest in untruth, our willful alliance with deception mars our God-concepts.

Though God is immutable, our concepts of Him are not. Our God-concepts are always in motion, and all our thoughts—purposefully chosen or passively permitted—affect that formation. Brother Lawrence, known for his intimacy with God, wrote, "The foundation of spiritual life, for me, has been a high image of God and a high esteem of God."[2]

What we choose to think matters, a lot.

⏸ GUIDED RESPONSE

Thought Focus:
Carry this request with you for several days: *God, reveal to me any area in which I'm watering thorns in my God-concept.* Be sensitive to

the Holy Spirit's gentle conviction alerting you to the nurturing of thoughts that mar the accuracy of God's portrait in your soul.

Exercise:

1. Set a timer to remind yourself at regular intervals (such as once every hour or two) to ask, *What comes into my mind when I think about God right now?* The purpose is to start noticing what, and if, we are thinking about God in various contexts: in the morning, after a tense call, when a project is running late, while paying bills, or when lonely.

2. Write down your answers in a notepad, journal, or directly onto the second canvas or cardstock.

   • For example, right now, at 7:30 p.m. on a Monday, what comes into my mind when I think about God is *present* and *mentor* because I have spent the day writing and listening. When I transition to relax with the family, check on the kids' homework, and try to get everyone to bed at a decent hour, I might write on my canvas: *patient*, *gracious*, and *laughing*.

   • Honest answers can also include *nothing*, *I don't know*, or *I'm not thinking about Him right now*. That is okay. Write the day, time, and *nothing* or *IDK*.

3. At day's end, reflect on your entries. Note anything you may be learning about yourself, your portrait of God, God Himself, or the relationship you share.

GOD IN THE ROOM

> *Pausing to honor my friend's tears, I softly asked,*
> *"Where's God?"*
>
> *"Excuse me?" she replied, rather puzzled.*
>
> *"Where's God in the picture? You've described the context,*
> *the conflict, yourself, the leader. I have a motion picture in my*
> *mind that's rolling from the clear depiction. I'm wondering*
> *about the placement of one more character in the story: God.*
> *In your memory, look around the scene. Where is He?"*
>
> *"Nowhere," she gasped with widening eyes. "He's not even*
> *in the room."*

Not even in the room.

Years later, my friend marks this revelation as a turning point in her spiritual journey. A faithful follower of Jesus, she worshiped God, consulted God, prayed to God, and served God. She was living her life 24/7 *for* God, but not 24/7 *with* God.

> Her official God-concept (that hung on the wall) said,
> "Present."
>
> Her working God-concept (that framed her memories)
> said, "Absent."

Not even in the room.

Sadly, we see God in precious few of the rooms in the archived memories of our pasts. It is therefore understandable, though still spiritually crippling, that we also rarely see Him in the rooms of our present.

If pressed in everyday moments to honestly answer Tozer's question—"What comes into my mind when I think about God?"— many, if not most, would confess that my friend's struggle feels all too real and familiar.

"Honestly, I don't know," we might admit.

"Quite frankly, nothing. I'm not thinking about Him," we would confess.

"Well, this morning I read," we would stretch.

"In a recent message I heard," we might punt.

The hesitation can have a multitude of sources:

- Monitoring inner thoughts—inclusive of our thoughts about God—can be a true struggle for some sincere souls.
- More than a few may have a degree of theological uncertainty regarding God's involvement, or even interest, in the details of our lives.
- Christian education has perhaps modeled a pattern of thinking *about* God more than thinking *with* God.
- In practice, many view God as a supportive coworker more than as the Lover of our souls and, consequently, excel at serving more than abiding.

Whatever the why, reality remains unchanged: see Him or not, God was—and still is—in the room.

The author of the book of Hebrews echoed ancient wisdom uttered by Moses to God's people in the Old Testament: "God has said, 'Never will I leave you; never will I forsake you'" (Hebrews 13:5).

God does not leave. God does not forsake. In every season, in every moment, God is in the room.

God-in-the-room transitions our souls from visiting a well to living in a spring.

God-in-the-room means that our angst about things that happened in His absence refocuses more accurately to angst about what happened in His presence.

God-in-the-room offers the certainty that whatever the story and wherever the wounds, we are never alone and we are always fully known.

God-in-the-room means each thought is heard, every tear is counted, all joys are shared, and no question is unwanted.

God-in-the-room opens the door for our Life-Maker to be our Life-Mentor.

God-in-the-room means that *Immanuel*—God with us—is more than a song.

So, what comes into your mind when you think about God?

⏸ GUIDED RESPONSE

Thought Focus:

Where is God in the room? Today, if you wince about the past, fret about the future, or wonder about the present, pause long enough to answer these questions: Where do you see God in the room? Is He close? Is He absent? Is His hand on your shoulder? What expression do you imagine is on His face? Use your God-given imagination to help you discover your working God-concepts.

Exercise:

This exercise adds others' perspectives of our God-concepts to our growing collection of God-portraits.

1. Identify three or four good friends, coworkers, family members, or neighbors with whom you interact regularly.
2. With a notepad in hand, ask these individuals for their first responses to some version of a few of these questions:
   - When I talk about God or pray, how do I refer to God? Do I pray to Jesus, the Holy Spirit, or the Father? Do I talk as though He is near or far away?
   - If my words were muted, from my attitudes and actions alone, what do you think I believe about God?
   - Which attributes of God do you think I treasure the most?
   - Is there anything about God that you think makes me uncomfortable?
3. On your third canvas or cardstock, represent these responses with a list of written words or a collage of images.
4. Consider what God-concepts permeate your life to the point that they are visible to others, and take time to journal your reflections.

13

THINKING BACKWARD

During a dark time of impending judgment in Israel's history, Isaiah penned these lines for a song of praise. The longed-for "perfect peace"—translated from שָׁלוֹם (shalom)—carries the meaning of completeness, soundness, and welfare.

> You will keep in perfect peace
>> those whose minds are steadfast,
>> because they trust in you.
> Trust in the LORD forever,
>> for the LORD, the LORD himself, is the Rock eternal.
>> (Isaiah 26:3–4)

God keeps our hearts peaceful (sound, complete, well) when we keep our minds trust-full (steadfast upon Him).

And trust—its absence or presence, its solidity or sponginess—is directly related to the health of our God-concepts.

> We cannot trust God in full if we believe He only loves
> us in part.
> We dare not trust God with our future if we believe
> that He was negligent in our past.

If, in our spiritual guts, we view God as inconsistent, absent, angry, or stingy, what we call "trust" may be a tentative half-dependence with a ready back-up plan, i.e., "I can only truly depend on myself."

God-concepts inform beliefs, and beliefs influence attitudes, emotions, and behaviors. The latter—attitudes, emotions, and behaviors—are followers, not leaders. They are responders, not initiators. As such, they are manifestations of something deeper in our working, applied belief systems.

Sometimes we may say, "I'm sorry I did/said that. I just wasn't thinking," which implies that we acted first and thought second. Though heartfelt, this is perhaps less than true. We probably *were* thinking. Our thinking may have been angry, selfish, poor, incorrect, incomplete, impulsive, or vengeful. But we *were* thinking.

Perhaps it is time to think *backward*: to start with the unpleasant attitude or unholy action and ask ourselves, *What in my thinking was justifying this attitude?*

When we fear the future, what does that reveal about our working God-concepts?

When we self-lead instead of wait, what do we really believe about God's goodness?

When we refuse to forgive ourselves, what does that reveal about our theology of Christ's crucifixion and resurrection?

When we fight for the oppressed one moment and then caress things Jesus died for the next, what does that disclose about our understanding of God's justice?

When we feel resentful toward life's scenery, what must we believe about God's sovereignty?

(You get the picture.)

Thinking backward awakens us to the why of our behaviors.

Thinking backward empowers us to discern and address unhealthy, unproductive misthinks in our God-concepts.

Thinking backward is a discipline by which we can retrain our minds.

The resulting healthier God-concepts will yield a sturdier, increasingly steadfast trust. Such trust is a must for those who long to live, whatever the scenery, in "perfect peace."

⏸ GUIDED RESPONSE

Thought Focus:

Try to think backward several times today. When you recognize an attitude or action that is not reflective of Jesus' character, think backward and ask what belief inspired the behavior: *God, help me understand what I was thinking deep within to have chosen and justified that attitude or action.*

Exercise:

1. Gather all three God-portrait canvases or cardstocks from the chapter 10, 11, and 12 exercises. Journal or pray your way through four steps.
2. Compare and contrast your chapter 10 and 11 canvases.
   - What attributes overlapped in both God-portraits?
   - What might contribute to the presence of non-overlapping attributes, i.e., attributes that only appeared in one or the other composite?
3. Compare and contrast your chapter 10 and 12 canvases.
   - What attributes overlapped in both God-portraits?
   - Spend a few moments listening to see if there is any dissonance between what you project to others and what you believe.
4. Compare and contrast your chapter 11 and 12 canvases.
   - What attributes overlapped in both God-portraits?

- Were you glad or sad about any descriptions of God in chapter 11 that did not show up in chapter 12?

5. From the composite of these three God-portraits, list any areas in your God-concept that you feel need refining or reconstruction.

[Movement Four]

SELF-CONCEPTS

> Jesus recognized with authentic realism that anyone who permits another to determine the quality of his inner life gives into the hands of the other the keys to his destiny.
>
> The awareness of being a child of God tends to stabilize the ego and results in a new courage, fearlessness, and power.[1]
>
> —HOWARD THURMAN, *JESUS AND THE DISINHERITED*

WHAT YOU WILL NEED FOR THE EXERCISES

✔ A notepad *or* journal
✔ Three or four wise and mature friends
✔ Tape
✔ A Bible

14

DOES GOD HAVE AN OPINION?

The alley behind my college dorm hosted midnight drug sales. Most of the time I steered clear, but every once in a while my study-filled, sleep-deprived brain would default to auto-pilot, and I would find myself walking through the alley after a late night at the library.

Though my heart would quicken, those buying and selling barely noticed me. With sadness, compassion, and anger I offered prayers while addicts injected poison into their bruised veins. Relieved faces could not hide reality: the poison was seducing their senses into the acceptance of a dark, new "normal" a million miles from truth.

Physically, most of us will never poison ourselves in this way.

Mentally, most of us habitually poison ourselves each day.

"I'm unattractive," we sigh.

"I'm all alone," we moan.

"I'm stupid," we wince.

"I'm worthless," we whisper.

"I've blown it," we decree.

"If only I were . . . ," we wish.

"If only I wasn't . . . ," we whimper.

"If only I hadn't . . . ," we regret.

And with each and every
self-rejecting thought

>we release a toxic syringe
>   into our veins.
>   And the poisonous thoughts
>   seduce us into accepting
>   a dark, new "normal"
>   a million miles from truth.

Why?

Why do we self-abuse by mentally self-poisoning?

Whether that "why" is sourced in merciless self-punishment for the past, twisted motivation for the future, the rotting fruit of someone else's sins against us, or a bitter lament over our own choices, it is time to soberly ask an eternally weighty question.

Does God have an opinion about our self-thoughts?

⓫ GUIDED RESPONSE

For the last four chapters, we have been discovering and examining our God-concepts. Now, standing on an ongoing commitment to compare our God-concepts with the Original, we turn our attention to discovering and examining our self-concepts from a biblical perspective.

Position yourself like an explorer heading into uncharted territory. For the moment, file away all your strengths tests, gifting inventories, leadership styles, and personality profiles.

We are going to collect fresh data.

Thought Focus:

For a set period of time (perhaps thirty minutes or an afternoon) keep track of how kind you are to yourself in your thoughts. For example:

- Looking in the mirror in the morning: *Oh well, this is as good as it's going to get.* (-1)
- Stepping into the car: *You know, you were patient with that neighbor this morning.* (+1)
- Realizing you left a needed report at home: *Ugh, I can reprint it, but I'm such an idiot.* (-1)

Exercise:

1. Throughout the next several days, take short notes capturing what you say *to* yourself *about* yourself and title it *Self-Concept Canvas 1.*

2. Include positive and negative thoughts from *I aced that presentation!* to *What's the use? I was just born fat.*

3. Place asterisks by anything you did not want to write down. But for now, avoid evaluation. Collect the real-time data, and let it sit.

15

SORTING THE MAIL

As a university student, the physical danger of the drugs in the back alley paled in comparison with the mental danger of the cloud in the classroom. The drug sales were periodically busted. But the proliferation of deception in the classroom was protected.

"Are any of you Christians?" one of my first English professors inquired. To the few of us who raised our hands, he said with confidence, "You won't be by the end of this class."

"Do any of you believe there's a God?" baited my tenured philosophy professor. "My goal is to have you certain of uncertainty by the time you graduate."

My first steps of faith were taken in an uneven environment that celebrated those who pursued truth and was offended by those who claimed to find truth. The great news, though, is that light is pretty easy to find in the dark.

And somewhere along the way, God led me into a glorious discovery: I do not have to think about what everyone wants me to think about. In other words, I can take authority over my mind.

This was a life-giving revelation.

As a compassionate artist, I felt that every suggestion, each question, and all proposed possibilities needed to be respected with equal time and attention. As an analytical academic, I assumed that intellectual integrity demanded the thorough consideration of opposing opinions and angst-laden arguments.

I was wrong.

True intellectual strength is not merely the ability *to* think. It is the ability to choose what to think and when to think.

Picture your mind as an exquisite desk stacked with mail. The fact that an envelope is on your desk neither forces you to open it nor obliges you to digest its contents. Giving every piece of mail equally meticulous attention would be distracting and exhausting.

Physically, we sort mail into a few piles:

- Trash
- Open, peruse, and trash
- File to consider later
- Immediate attention required

Spiritually, we must take the same authority.

As thoughts audition for attention via memories, our senses, friends' suggestions, strangers' assertions, or media's messaging, we need to sort the mail.

Even when given endless attention, mental junk mail will never evolve into wisdom.

⦿ GUIDED RESPONSE

Thought Focus:

As thoughts vie for attention in your mental space, sort the mail. Take authority over your mind: choose to trash mental junk mail and then resist the urge to go back and sort through the bin.

Exercise:

As we did with our God-portraits in chapter 12, we will now add to our self-portraits a layer of others' impressions.

1. Reach out to the three or four wise, self-controlled, close friends you identified earlier in *The Sacred Slow*.
2. Explain that you are on a journey to align your thoughts with God's thoughts and ask them if they have ever heard you say anything about yourself (positive or negative) that concerned them.
3. Give them a couple of days to respond, permission to be honest, and an assurance that you will not be defensive or say anything other than "thank you" for their comments.
4. Collect their contributions in a journal or notepad and title the page *Self-Concept Canvas 2*. As with the last chapter, to the best of your ability let the data gather without analysis.

NEW RULES, NEW START

Once upon a time . . .[1]

A generous soul lived an overly accessible life in a visitor-thick neighborhood.

> At first she felt loved (which was nice).
> Later she felt used (which was not so nice).
> And then she felt like just another piece of furniture (which was not nice at all).

You see, in the beginning, when the neighborhood knocked on her door, she welcomed each visitor into the warm space she called home. After all, generosity is a virtue, most visits lasted only a few minutes, and she rather enjoyed not being alone.

Over the years, their voices became familiar and their visits became part of her daily rhythm. She happily stocked her fridge with juice and her kitchen with treats. "Just grabbing a soda!" a voice would announce as the front door creaked open. "Thanks for the dessert!" another voice would shout as the back door slammed shut.

Then suddenly, one unsuspecting day, she woke up wondering what distinguished a visitor from an intruder. And so she sat in her chair and watched while dozens came and dozens left, each barely glancing at her. As the hours passed, she began to feel startled and helpless and more than a little alarmed as the truth dawned on her:

in her attempt to be generous, she had given away authority over her home.

Something drastic had to be done. So the generous soul who lived an overly accessible life in a visitor-thick neighborhood decided to rewrite the rules.

The hidden key had been willingly un-hid years before. Gathering up the keys, she called a locksmith and in one decisive afternoon changed all the locks.

And, she thought, *that settles that! New day. New rules. New start. Everyone else will catch on quickly.*

With a smile she closed the front door.
With a sigh she breathed in the silence.
And within what seemed like one minute, the doorbell began to ring.

She had hoped that the visitors would take polite notice of the obviously altered policy. She had hoped they would try the door, respect her decision, and quietly dismiss themselves. She had hoped in vain.

Their anger surprised her. As she hid inside her not-remotely-silent home, visitors knocked and banged and yelled, and she thought, *It was quieter before I changed the locks. It would have been easier to leave everything the way it was.*

And she was right.

But each time she was tempted to throw the new keys outside—like a bone to appease barking dogs—she remembered the alarming helplessness of forfeited authority and decided to stand her ground one more day.

Weeks passed, then months. The weaker voices grew weary and left first. The stronger voices grew louder and more demanding. However, the locksmith's work could not be undone by noise alone.

Then one day it occurred to her that she could hear *nothing*: no banging, no shouting, not even a persistent knock.

The word whispered in the visitor-thick neighborhood was finally confirmed: "All-access" has been revoked. The generous soul's warm space at the end of the road is entered *by invitation only*.

❙❙ GUIDED RESPONSE

Thought Focus:

Imagine that all the thoughts you permit in your mind are physical guests in a house. Whether fearful, proud, happy, discouraging, tidy, or unclean . . . each thought takes on a persona reflective of its nature. Are there any "guests" you would want to dismiss, hide, or make excuses for if you were giving someone you spiritually respect an all-access tour of your headspace?

Exercise:

1. Place self-concept canvases 1 and 2 in front of you, and quiet your mind in God's presence. Then ask, *Savior, is there anything on these canvases that grieves You?* (Such a prayer initiates a God-search as opposed to a self-led evaluation.)

2. Repeat this prayer for a few days. If the Holy Spirit does not bring anything to your attention, thank God for His faithful work and continue with your day.

3. If God does bring something to your attention, enter into a brief time of uncomplicated and uncluttered repentance. For example, perhaps you sense God saying, *I am grieved, My son, that you so often belittle your contributions.* Respond with the following:

   • Acknowledge before God whether you had any prior knowledge that these thoughts grieved Him.

- Forgive (and keep forgiving) those who may have contributed to the formation of this misthink.
- Ask God's forgiveness for thinking less of yourself than He thinks of you.
- Thank Him for forgiving you and choose to forgive yourself.

CHANGING THE LOCKS

But each time she was tempted to throw the new keys
outside—like a bone to appease barking dogs—she
remembered the alarming helplessness of forfeited authority
and decided to stand her ground one more day.

This image of forfeited authority in the name of generosity
is startling. Clearly, the intrusive neighbors are symbolic of our
intrusive thoughts. Granting every thought that comes to mind all-
access entrance into our lives is neither generous nor integral; it is
self-sabotage.

This is serious. This is war. The angry response of the intruders
in the story mirrors the battle that *will* ensue as we change the locks
in our minds and purpose to assert authority over our thought-life.

Thought is the founder of legacy.
Words shape us.
Head-talk forms us.

An undisciplined mind undermines the pursuit of intimacy
with God.

What if we solemnly committed to the slow, lifelong retraining of our minds? What if we established mental checkpoints with
standards to screen our thoughts? What if the number one rule in

that standard was asking God's opinion about our thoughts *before* we passively or actively invested another second in them?

Imagine what could happen in one month by our choice just to enter the battle. Imagine what could happen in a year as less crowded (and less toxic) conditions free up our mental and emotional resources. Imagine what could happen in one decade as we collectively "take captive every thought to make it obedient to Christ" (2 Corinthians 10:5).

Imagine the fear in the Enemy's eyes that we are even having this discussion. Yes, *fear*.

The kingdom of darkness has everything to fear if it loses its hidden ground of guerilla warfare in our heads. There, camouflaged by busyness, arrogance, self-pity, or shame, it skillfully turns us against ourselves to degrees that range from distracting to destructive.

Untruth has never been neutral.

Practically, changing the locks in our minds can begin with two steps:

1. Next time a thought presses our minds for entrance, pause long enough to ask, *Can I think this thought* with *Jesus?* If so, wonderful. Whether comforting or corrective, think with God in the room.
2. If not, let the battle begin: treat such thoughts as intruders and their nurturing as disobedience.

Personally, in that battle, my goal is neither to deny the struggle nor to hyper-focus on the struggle (e.g., by journaling reasons why this particular untruth is attractive to me). Instead, I derail the untruth by jumping tracks. Here are a few of my favorite weapons:

- I begin praying—by name or by group—for those who do not yet know Jesus. Frankly, if the enemy is going to attempt to torment or tempt me, I am going to fight back where it will hurt the kingdom of darkness the most. Instead of bemoaning my vulnerability, I exercise my authority to intercede for the lost Jesus is seeking to save.

- I recall and recite whatever passage I am currently meditating on or memorizing.
- Aloud I declare, "Those aren't my Savior's thoughts toward me. He says that I am _____" and I fill in the blank with scripture.

Perhaps part of the reason we approach this battle timidly is because internally we are divided. Deep in our hearts we believe that meditating on untruth has benefits. Once we abandon the deception that we can manage untruth to our advantage, we can, with force and freedom, change the locks and stand firm.

⏸ GUIDED RESPONSE

Thought Focus:
Reconsider the last paragraph several times. Is there any area of your thought-life that is overdue for a lock change?

Exercise:
1. Look over self-concept canvases 1 and 2, and circle anything that is toxic.
2. Meditating on Scripture is a powerful antidote for toxic thinking. The Word extracts poison and inserts truth. Commit to looking up several of the following scriptures daily. As you read, ask, "What would change if I really believed this were true about me?"
   - *Who Am I?*
     Matthew 5:13, 14

John 1:12; 15:1, 5, 15, 16

Romans 6:18, 22; 8:14, 15, 17

1 Corinthians 1:2; 3:16; 6:17, 19; 12:27; 15:10

2 Corinthians 5:17, 18, 19

Galatians 3:26, 28; 4:6, 7

Ephesians 1:1; 2:6, 10, 19; 3:1; 4:1, 24; 5:30

Philippians 1:1; 3:20

Colossians 3:3, 4, 12

1 Thessalonians 1:4, 5

Hebrews 3:1, 14

1 Peter 2:5, 9, 10, 11; 5:8

1 John 3:1, 2; 5:18

- *Since I am in Christ, by the grace of God:*
  Romans 5:1; 6:1–6; 8:1

  1 Corinthians 1:30; 2:12, 16; 6:19, 20

  2 Corinthians 1:21; 5:14, 15, 21

  Galatians 2:20

  Ephesians 1:3, 4, 5, 7, 13–14; 2:5, 6, 18; 3:12

  Colossians 1:13, 14, 27; 2:7, 10, 11, 12, 13; 3:1–4

  2 Timothy 1:7, 9

  Titus 3:5

  Hebrews 2:11; 4:16

  2 Peter 1:4[1]

CENTRALIZING HIS PRESENCE

A PRAYER OF STABILITY

Brother Jesus, . . .
Free me from my restless activity,
my slavery to the clock,
my habit of bobbing along on the open sea
when you have called me to be still.
When I consider how you consented to enclosure
in Mary's womb,
in a narrow manger,
on the wooden cross,
my heart is moved to seek enclosure with you. Amen.[1]
—GLORIA HUTCHINSON, *SIX WAYS TO*
PRAY FROM SIX GREAT SAINTS

WHAT YOU WILL NEED FOR THE EXERCISES

✔ Walking shoes
✔ A notepad *or* journal
✔ Access to a few souls who walk closely with God
✔ A Bible

FAITH AS A DUET

The effort we have exerted over the past eight chapters to take captive every God-thought and self-thought to make it obedient to Christ (2 Corinthians 10:5) has prepared us for this next movement in our Sacred Slow journey.

As I mentioned in the last chapter, head-talk is formative.

> We whisper, "You are never alone," to frightened children.
> We offer, "God is with you," to grieving souls.
> We affirm, "Your Savior is near," to the lonely.
> And then proceed *to live alone* in our heads.

Why?

Why do we engage in God-talk in the morning and during times of prayer, but then engage in self-talk the rest of the day? God invites us into a continuous duet, but in practice we live most of our lives as a solo.

On the surface, we may say that something is "too small to bother God with," or we may avoid the duet in the name of accepting personal responsibility "because God gave us a brain." However, at the root, perhaps the true issue is whether or not we believe that God is equally present in every moment.

Is He with us, or is He just observing us?

Is Christ in us as "the hope of glory," or is Christ
simply aware of us as a manifestation of His omniscience?
Our answer will affect our communion.

We recognize the value of devotions and quiet times. However,
these spaces are means to an end, not ends in and of themselves. God
Himself is our end and our beginning. God Himself is our destina-
tion and companion. As Oswald Chambers said, "My goal is God
Himself: not joy nor peace nor even blessing, but Himself my God."[1]

Trusting God as our Good Shepherd is wise. And there
is more.
Depending on God as our present help is strength.
And there is more.
Following God as our Wonderful Counselor is
surrender. And there is more.
Jesus, our Messiah, is Immanuel, which means that
God is *with* us.[2]

A whole lot of power is packed in that little preposition. *With*
means "that people or things are together in one place" or "that two or
more people are doing something together or involved in something."[3]
Through the door opened by Jesus' sacrifice, you and God
are together in one place. In everything you do, God is with you.
Centralizing His presence means that we willfully discipline our
souls to grow in attentiveness to the One who is continually with us.
Countless faithful believers who have gone before us affirm
that it *is* possible—even in this distracting world—to centralize our
earthly existence in God.
Although *Merriam-Webster*'s first definition of *center* (referencing geometry) has meaningful implications,[4] the second definition
more obviously relates to our focus:

cen·ter *noun* \'sen-tər,'se-nər\

> 2a: a point, area, person, or thing that is most important or pivotal in relation to an indicated activity, interest, or condition
>
> 2b: a source from which something originates[5]

On the ground, what does it mean to centralize His presence? How do we cultivate a life in which our thoughts *pivot* on God and our actions *originate* in God's nearness?

 ## GUIDED RESPONSE

Thought Focus:

Pick a common occurrence in your daily life such as waiting at a traffic light, being asked a question, or the ring of a phone. Then each time the event occurs, take a quick inventory: *Am I engaged in a duet with God or a solo with myself in my thoughts?* If your answer is "a solo," simply include God in the conversation.

Exercise:

1. Personalize this prayer: *God, be my center. Show me how to discipline my thoughts to pivot on You. Reveal how I can transition my actions from originating in my head to originating near Your heart.*

2. For a few minutes, hold this prayer in your thoughts as you would a wildflower: with gentle attentiveness. In other words, do not be anxious for an answer. Merely focus on relationship.

3. Take this prayer with you and go on a walk outside with Jesus.

4. Take note of details in God's creation and talk with Him about them. Tell Him things He already knows as opposed to pondering things alone in your head. Purpose to converse.

5. As you walk with Jesus, repeat the refrain from C. Austin Miles's 1913 hymn:

And He walks with me, and He talks with me,
And He tells me I am His own.
And the joy we share as we tarry there,
None other has ever known[6]

19

OUR PRIMARY OCCUPATION

Jesus went up on a mountainside and called to him those
he wanted, and they came to him. He appointed twelve
that they might be with him and that he might send them
out to preach and to have authority to drive out demons.
(Mark 3:13–15)

Jesus gave the Twelve a job description containing three
responsibilities:

1. Be with Jesus—stay with Him at all times.
2. Be sent out by Jesus—carry to others the messages you will
   learn from being in relationship with Him.
3. Exercise authority from Jesus—overcome obstacles with the
   authority He will give to you.

In order, *go* and *do* are positioned as successors, not predecessors,
of *be*. Public service for Christ is the fruit—not the root—of personal
relationship with Christ.

How consistent for Immanuel, God with us, to make being with
Him our primary occupation.

Jesus' "be with me" was literal. He said, "Come, follow Me," and
from the disciples' "yes" forward, they became His companions. They
were together in the city, in the country, and on all the roads in between.
They stayed with Jesus in homes, in the temple, and in the synagogues.

They walked with Jesus, fished with Jesus, served with Jesus, and survived storms with Jesus. *With*-ship was their priority calling.

In the words of Brother Lawrence, the disciples "practiced the presence" of Christ 24/7:

> I cannot imagine how a Christian can live a satisfied Christian experience without the practice of being in the presence of Christ. For my part, I keep myself retired with Him in the center of my soul as much as I can. While I am with Him I fear nothing.[1]

"Well, that would be more realistic for us if we—like the Twelve— could see Jesus' face," we say with a sigh. Perhaps this objection was, in part, what Jesus had in mind as He addressed the disciples at the ascension:

> Then Jesus came to them and said, "All authority in heaven and on earth has been given to me. Therefore go and make disciples of all nations, baptizing them in the name of the Father and of the Son and of the Holy Spirit, and teaching them to obey everything I have commanded you. And surely I am with you always, to the very end of the age." (Matthew 28:18–20)

The job description in Mark 3 and the Great Commission in Matthew 28 bookend and mirror each other. They contain the same elements in reverse. In Mark 3, Jesus spoke of being with Him, sending them out to preach, and giving them authority. In Matthew 28, Jesus spoke of having authority, described their role as sent ones, and ended with a promise of His presence.

In the beginning of His earthly ministry, Jesus said, "Be with me." At the end of His earthly ministry, Jesus said, "I am with you," as though Jesus were responding to His disciples' objections before they could even be verbalized.

No longer would they see His face, but Jesus assured them (and us) that He would be as present as He had ever been.

Present.
Jesus is with us.

Which means almost two thousand years after that first call, the priority job description of a Jesus-follower is still literal.

 GUIDED RESPONSE

Thought Focus:

Read John 11:1–44 and picture yourself in the story as one of Jesus' disciples. Imagine what it might have felt like to walk in physical proximity with Jesus. Then remember His promise: "I will be with you always."

Exercise:

1. Continue to hold the prayer found at the end of chapter 18 before the Lord and journal any directives or impressions that come to mind: *God, be my center. Show me how to discipline my thoughts to pivot on You. Reveal how I can transition my actions from originating in my head to originating near Your heart.*

2. Now add research to your pursuit of centralizing the presence of God. Recall the list of individuals whom you perceive walk near God. Ask yourself, "What is it about these souls that led me to choose them?" Then contact them and, respecting whatever time frame they have offered, ask these questions with a recorder running or your fingers flying on a keyboard:
   • What is your definition of intimacy with God?

- What disciplines, practices, or attitudes have helped you cultivate nearness with God?
- What are my/our generation's greatest hindrances to truly living with God as the center of all we do, say, and are?

20

INVITED HOME

What can a disciple's primary occupation of *being with Jesus* look like in our day?

Consider another echo of this priority calling from John 15:4. Knowing of His imminent crucifixion, resurrection, and ascension, Jesus said to His disciples, "Remain in me, as I also remain in you."

Does *being with Him* and *remaining in Him* mean that we should

- Move into a monastery?
- Sit in silence on a mountaintop?
- Memorize every red letter in the Bible?
- Copy the Gospels by hand onto papyrus?
- Move to Israel and retrace Christ's steps?
- Abandon family ties and become recluses?
- Do nothing until we discern His impressions?

Though some of these possibilities may at times sound attractive (especially on noisy, cluttered days), making our home in Jesus—being with Him—is less about physical geography and more about spiritual gravity. Remaining in Jesus is less about external activity and more about interior attentiveness.

The Greek word that is translated *remain* in John 15 is μένω (menō), which most often appears as "to stay, abide, or remain." *The*

Message Bible interprets Jesus' words in John 15:4 as, "Live in me. Make your home in me just as I do in you."

Mystery of mysteries, Christ is *in* those who make Him their home (Colossians 1:27). When we believe that Jesus' sacrifice and resurrection reconciles us to the Father, the Holy Spirit makes His home in our spirit. God's breath both created and sustains our spirit, and that spirit was always meant to be His home.

We think of God as out there, somewhere, and search for Him as though He were lost. In reality, our omnipresent Creator is "out there" and also "in here." Christ is within. So being with God and remaining in Him are awakening to and exploring forever the biblical truth that we are God's resting place.

I wonder if part of our sleepiness toward interpreting Jesus' "I will remain in you" plainly is related to the world's deadly distortions of that truth. Given the ancient, yet newly packaged, deception that we are all gods and that we need to discover the divine within, it seems safer to picture God as *outside* and self as *inside*.

However, *interaction* has never been a synonym for *fusion*.

God abides in our spirit, *and* our spirit is
not God.

God speaks to us and through us, *but* God will
never be us.

We are creation and God is Creator. Even given
an eternity of time, the pot cannot evolve into the
Potter.

The Lover of our souls awaits us. Each moment of every day is overflowing with an invitation to abide in Christ. We can always "be with Him" because He has made His home in us.

He longs for us to live present to His presence.

⓫ GUIDED RESPONSE

Thought Focus:

Consider the personal implications of Jesus' promise ("I am in you") from John 14:15–20.

> If you love me, keep my commands. And I will ask the Father, and he will give you another advocate to help you and be with you forever—the Spirit of truth. The world cannot accept him, because it neither sees him nor knows him. But you know him, for he lives with you and will be in you. I will not leave you as orphans; I will come to you. Before long, the world will not see me anymore, but you will see me. Because I live, you also will live. On that day you will realize that I am in my Father, and you are in me, and I am in you.

Exercise:

The potential of centralizing the presence of God is breathtaking. Now we will make practical what could easily remain poetry and develop a plan to discipline our minds and spirits.

1. Gather your notes and reflections from chapters 18 and 19. Review them prayerfully, circling possibilities that are most appealing to you in this season.
2. Systematically experiment with different options. For example:
   - Make Jesus' priority calling—"Be with Me"—a screen saver. Each time it appears, pause to whisper *"I love You"* or *"You are with me"* to your Savior.
   - Tie a string around your finger (do not laugh—this will be gold for some). Let it remind you to think *with* God and not just to yourself, e.g., *Lord, this meeting could get tense. I'm so glad we go into it together.*

- Set your phone alarm at regular intervals to remind you to picture God at home in your spirit.
- Post Jesus' words all over your house. Let them prompt you to move toward a continual conversation with God about His Word.
- Try to do little things for the love of God.[1] When you drive to work, eat, wash a dish, or pay a bill, thank God for the strength to drive, work, eat, wash, and pay. Transform common acts into sincere love offerings to God.

As you focus with intention on these exercises, consider these words from Brother Lawrence:

In the way of God, thoughts count for little, love does everything. And it is not necessary to have great things to do. I turn my little omelet in the pan for the love of God; when it is finished, if I have nothing to do, I prostrate myself on the ground and adore my God, who gave me the grace to make it, after which I arise, more content than a king.[2]

[2 1]

INHERITANCE PRAYERS

Apart from wisdom for this challenge, guidance for that project, healing for your body, peace for a relationship, provision for a need, and protection for the future, what do you pray *for yourself*?

The Scriptures are all precious to me. I truly love to study and pray God's Word. But over the years, three passages have consistently shot out of the pages like a skilled arrow into the center of my soul. Months or even years may pass, but when I stumble upon these verses again, I am stunned anew by how these ancient words feel immediately personal. Though rare, the experience always brings tears to my eyes, and for a few seconds, I become physically aware of what is always true: God is holy, and His Word is living.

For a long time, I had gratitude but little understanding of these moments until one day when I kept reading past the conclusion of a book into the appendices.[1] There, in appendix 5 of a thin book on prayer by Graham Cooke, the following words mentored me:

> Ask God for an inheritance word. These are usually passages of Scripture that He highlights. . . . He will put it in your heart, and it is your inheritance. . . . Study it. Look it up in Bible commentaries. Research the original language. Ask God to illuminate His truth in it. . . . This passage is part of the conversation in heaven about you. Then write a crafted prayer about it.[2]

And so I did. Alongside the scripture-prayers I crafted for my family, I began to pray these scriptures over my life. Such prayers are customized not for a specific moment or a certain crisis but for our *existence*. They help us centralize the presence of God by honoring the Word of God applied to our lives.

In addition to my real-time requests based on the whole of Scripture (e.g., *God, You are a light to my feet and a lamp to my path in this conflict at work*), I began to unfurl inheritance prayers like a mighty flag over my life.

The focus of such prayers—from originating foundation (in God's Word) to verbalized declaration (over our lives)—is intimacy with God.

Barry and I steward a prayer retreat home that is graced with original art. Each artist named his or her work based on what he or she intended, experienced, and saw during the creative process. Likewise, God has named you as the work of His hands! Do you know what was in His heart when He crafted you?

God had tears of love in His eyes as He formed you in the womb. You are saturated with His fingerprints. Therefore, boldly ask God what was on His mind when He designed you.

I consider myself to be an infant in the crafting of such prayers. But I will offer you one of my own based on Jeremiah 30:21–22 and Exodus 33:11 as an example in the hope that it may inspire your journey:

> *Savior of my soul, draw me near.*
> *I long to live each breath close to You.*
> *I devote myself to being close to You.*
> *I am Yours and You are mine.*
> *Speak to me, Lord.*
> *Speak to me face-to-face.*
> *Speak to me as You would a friend.*
> *Let every word I offer to others come from Your presence.*

And my God, may those whom I invest in never, ever leave Your tent.

⑪ GUIDED RESPONSE

Thought Focus:
Hold this question in prayer: *My good and generous Father, what are Your thoughts toward me?*

Exercise:
1. Take a set of deep breaths. Reread this chapter aloud, aware of the Lord's presence.
2. Use your God-given imagination to picture Him as your original Artist. See Him painting you as His masterpiece. Consider Him at a potter's wheel forming you into His priceless vessel.
3. With your Bible open, ask: *Beloved Savior, what was in Your heart when You created me?*
4. Wait, listen, and write fragments of thoughts, images, and pictures that come to mind.
5. Ask God to direct you to scriptures that reflect His heart for you. These may be verses you have treasured for years or verses you are reading for the first time. Whatever their history, these are the verses that touch something deep within you.
6. Then craft a prayer based on these scriptures and impressions. Keep it focused. Make every word count.

Keep this draft near and dear. In the coming days, add further insights to this inheritance prayer. Every time you release these words, think of that mighty flag unfurling as a declaration of God's fierce love for you.

RELATING TO HIS WORD

> [The Devil] has a gospel without any repentance, without any obedience, without any cross-carrying, without any restitution-making, without holy living, and with a sort of heaven at the end. . . . I teach no adaptation of the Gospel. I will keep the blessed Gospel whole, as it is; but I contend we may serve it up on any sort of dish that will induce the people to partake of it.[1]
>
> —CATHERINE BOOTH, *CATHERINE BOOTH: A BIOGRAPHY OF THE COFOUNDER OF THE SALVATION ARMY*

WHAT YOU WILL NEED FOR THE EXERCISES

✔ A Bible
✔ Access to Bible study tools
✔ A text-only copy of John 14–17 (in the Toolbox)
✔ A notepad *or* journal
✔ A highlighter *or* colored pencils

THE WORD

The following was penned by a practical fisherman, not by a poetic philosopher:

> In the beginning was the Word, and the Word was with God, and the Word was God. He was with God in the beginning. (John 1:1–2)

By profession, the fisherman made his living from things tangible and tradable. By appointment, the fisherman/apostle was invited to see into the heavenlies:

> His eyes are like blazing fire, and on his head are many crowns. He has a name written on him that no one knows but he himself. He is dressed in a robe dipped in blood, and his name is the Word of God. The armies of heaven were following him, riding on white horses and dressed in fine linen, white and clean. (Revelation 19:12–14)

What John saw on earth and in heaven was the Word:

The same Word we call Creator, whose breath ignited the universe.

The same Word we call Savior, whose blood was spilled for our sins.

The same Word we call Victor, whose return will shake the nations.

The Word heard became Immanuel, and His holy story was carried by its hearers from generation to generation: treasured, taught, and transferred from voice to ear, pen to papyrus, printing press to paper, and digital code to digital device.

In our culture, the Word heard has become so common that it is often found on the floor next to dirty shoes, in the back of vans dusted with crushed breakfast cereal, and in phones buried under endless apps. Yes, physically the Bible is just a book. But the pages of this book contain echoes of the Eternal Voice.

Something is amiss. Perhaps access has led to apathy?

Something has been lost. Perhaps familiarity has bred contempt?

Something must be found. Something of honor and reverence.

Because somehow, King David's "Your word is a lamp for my feet" (Psalm 119:105) has deteriorated into "Your Word is optional to my faith-walk."

The Word is one of the greatest gifts entrusted to souls pursuing nearness with God. We are unspeakably fortunate to live in an age where His Word is in our hands. In previous centuries—and still in some persecuted spaces on earth—people have paid with their lives for the joy of holding even a fragment of the Bible.

As we embark on this new movement in *The Sacred Slow*, place the Word in your hands. Consider this quote from Tricia McCary Rhodes about reading the Bible, and ask, *What do I really believe is in this book?*

Take time to be thoughtful and prayerful. Remember that you are not interacting with words, but with God Himself.[1]

(II) GUIDED RESPONSE

Thought Focus:

Take an inventory of your Bibles. Whether paper, phone, audio, or digital, each day hold the Bible in your hands and ask, "What do I really believe about God's Word?"

Exercise:

Glorious! We are going to devote five exercises to studying the Word together. For some, these exercises will be as familiar as this morning's devotional. For others, these practices may be the first steps of a new and transformational discipline.

1. John 14–17 will be our focus. Pick up your Bible and pray. Thank God for the gift you hold in your hands. Ask the Holy Spirit to teach you and to lead you into truth.
2. Consult the Gospels, a study Bible, a Bible dictionary, or an online Bible study resource[2] to learn about the historical context of John's gospel.
   - *Who* was John?
   - *When* and *from where* did John write this gospel?
   - *To whom* and *for whom* was the gospel of John written?
   - If possible to discern, *why* did John write this gospel?
3. Frame John 14–17 in the broader context of the gospel of John.
   - These are red-letter chapters, consisting of Jesus' teaching and Jesus' prayer. What happened immediately prior to John 14? Immediately following John 17?

- Chronologically, are these chapters toward the beginning or the end of Jesus' public ministry?
- Who is Jesus speaking to as John 14 begins?

4. Picture John the fisherman/apostle and the life he lived. Then imagine him writing Jesus' story for future generations. What might Spirit-inspired writing have looked like?

A KITE WITHOUT A STRING

He was hipster-casual and personable. He had worked hard to make his hair look like he had not touched it for days. He was twentysomething, intelligent, and oblivious.

"So, you write books? That's cool," he said as the flight attendant repeated to the next passenger that they stopped serving peanuts years ago.

"What do you write about?" he asked. I love this question, especially on long flights, because it has often opened the door to rich discussion.

As our conversation continued, it became clear that we had a lot in common. We were both concerned about the environment, committed to social justice and organic living, artistic in spirit, and followers of Jesus.

My husband and I treasure this age group and have devoted vast chunks of our lives to mentoring them. But while Twentysomething affirmed how cool Jesus was, I had a sense that something was off-center. His eyes were a bit cloudy, but my primary concern was his soul.

I felt like I was speaking to a kite without a string: brilliantly colored, riding the winds, and in no one's hands. He lacked that glorious tension of being grounded.

Kites are not connected to the earth by unbendable metal poles (otherwise they would be called flags) or even by thick, rigid wires.

Kites are connected via string to a guiding hand and will. Without that string—without that guiding and grounding tension—kites are at the mercy of whichever way the wind blows until they become too stuck or too broken to move.

"Yeah," he continued, "I love Jesus. I'm not into the Bible at all. I'm just into Jesus."

My left eyebrow rose against my will. "Wow. What are your thoughts about the Bible?" I inquired.

"Like any other book . . . inconsistencies . . . can't know what really happened . . ."

As a former atheist, these comments are familiar to me. I used them against Christians to dismiss their faith as based on fairy tales. As a follower of Jesus, however, these "heard it from someone else but never exerted the effort to study it myself" responses grant me an opportunity to practice controlled breathing.

Some people are truly unable to read or hear the Word because of illiteracy, illness, physical disability, mental inability, or absent opportunity. I have met such souls. But here was a man who had access and freedom that millions only dream of, who could see and read and hear, who had the intelligence to study and even teach, and who was dismissing the Bible with one cool flick of his wrist.

A kite without a string.

The Word grounds our spirituality. It creates a healthy tension for our practiced theology. The Word connects our lives with a timeless community of faith. It gives us history and a future because it is simultaneously ancient and new every day.

So, what happened on the plane? Well, I wanted to say, "Please, be anything but apathetic. Wrestle with your doubts. Ask all the questions you want. But don't passively acquiesce to a sloppy, cynical dismissal." Thankfully, the Holy Spirit intervened.

Over the next hour of our conversation, I actively listened, gently questioned, and calmly shared how the Word, to me, is the Voice, how it stands up well to literary and historical criticism, how God is not nervous when we have questions, how out of respect for the *billions* who believe the Bible is God's Word, humility invites us to consider carefully our conclusions about the Scriptures.

His response? "Cool for you."

And he floated off the plane.

⓫ GUIDED RESPONSE

Thought Focus:

Read Psalm 19:7–11 below. Then look beyond the poetic beauty of David's psalm and attempt to rephrase each sentence in your own words.

> The law of the Lord is perfect,
> 　　refreshing the soul.
> The statutes of the Lord are trustworthy,
> 　　making wise the simple.
> The precepts of the Lord are right,
> 　　giving joy to the heart.
> The commands of the Lord are radiant,
> 　　giving light to the eyes.
> The fear of the Lord is pure,
> 　　enduring forever.
> The decrees of the Lord are firm,
> 　　and all of them are righteous.
>
> They are more precious than gold,
> 　　than much pure gold;
> They are sweeter than honey,
> 　　than honey from the honeycomb.

By them your servant is warned;

in keeping them there is great reward.

Exercise:

1. Pick up your Bible and pray. Thank God for the gift you hold in your hands. Ask the Holy Spirit to teach you and lead you into truth.

2. Review your research from chapter 22. Turn to the text-only copy of John 14–17 in the Toolbox at the back of this book. Read these chapters aloud and write down any reflections.

3. With a highlighter or colored pencils, silently read these chapters once more. Circle, underline, or highlight the following:
   - Broad themes
   - Repeated words, phrases, and images
   - Commands and exhortations
   - "I am" statements of Jesus
   - Frequent sentence constructions, such as *if . . . then* statements, that are literal or implied

4. As you read, place paragraph marks where you sense that a thought is completed. Without referencing your Bible, give titles to these emerging sections.

TO GOD ABOUT GOD'S WORD

Psalm 119 is remarkable. All but 2 of its 176 verses rejoice over God's Word.

> This celebrated psalm has several peculiarities. It is divided into twenty-two parts or stanzas, denoted by the twenty-two letters of the Hebrew alphabet. Each stanza contains eight verses, and the first letter of each verse is that which gives name to the stanza. Its contents are mainly praises of God's Word, exhortations to its perusal, and reverence for it, prayers for its proper influence, and complaints of the wicked for despising it.[1]

Most Jewish scholars have historically leaned toward King David as the probable psalmist of this "orphaned psalm"—one in which the author is not identified in the text.[2] Though David's life would unquestionably infuse additional meaning into each sentence, since its authorship is uncertain, I will consider Psalm 119 from the perspective of an anonymous pen.

A profound pen,
> that treasured God's words
> > before "the Word became flesh and made his dwelling
> > among us" (John 1:14).
Pre-incarnation,

pre-resurrection, and
    pre–printing press:
an anonymous pen,
    that blended faith and art,
      to create a masterpiece that it did not sign.

Psalm 119 is written to God about God's Word. When studying the psalm, three categories of content stood out to me: the psalmist's *relationship* with God's Word, descriptions of the *power* of God's Word, and *prayers* about God's Word.

Relationship is a key concept. We *use* things that are dead but *relate* to things that are living. We may use a computer, but we must relate to the Bible because the Word of God is alive.[3]

The list below is a compilation of what this anonymous pen said to God about his relationship with God's Word, starting with the most often repeated concepts.

Resist the urge to scan these verses quickly.

Instead, as you read each line ask yourself, "What would I have to believe to write this sentence with integrity and enthusiasm?"

- I will obey Your decrees. (eleven times)[4]
- I love Your commands. (ten times)[5]
- I meditate on Your precepts. (seven times)[6]
- I will not forget Your law. (six times)[7]
- I delight in Your decrees. (five times)[8]
- I keep Your statutes. (five times)[9]
- I have put my hope in Your law. (five times)[10]
- My soul is consumed with longing for Your laws at all times. (three times)[11]
- I do not turn from Your law. (three times)[12]
- My heart is set on keeping Your decrees to the very end. (two times)[13]
- I have sought out Your precepts. (two times)[14]

- I have not departed from Your laws. (two times)[15]
- I will follow Your righteous laws. (two times)[16]
- I learn Your righteous laws. (v. 7)
- I have hidden Your Word in my heart. (v. 11)
- With my lips I recount all the laws that come from Your mouth. (v. 13)
- I rejoice in following Your statutes. (v. 14)
- I will not neglect Your Word. (v. 16)
- I have set my heart on Your laws. (v. 30)
- I run in the path of Your commands. (v. 32)
- I trust in Your Word. (v. 42)
- I will speak of Your statutes before kings. (v. 46)
- I remember, Lord, Your ancient laws. (v. 52)
- I find comfort in them [Your ancient laws]. (v. 52)
- Your decrees are the theme of my song. (v. 54)
- I have turned my steps to Your statutes. (v. 59)
- I trust in Your commands. (v. 66)
- I will ponder Your statutes. (v. 95)
- I gain understanding from Your precepts. (v. 104)
- I will always have regard for Your decrees. (v. 117)
- I stand in awe of Your laws. (v. 120)
- I consider all Your precepts right. (v. 128)
- My heart trembles at Your Word. (v. 161)
- I have chosen Your precepts. (v. 173)

Such was the uncommon commitment of an anonymous pen to the Word pre-incarnate.

❚❚ GUIDED RESPONSE

Thought Focus:

In Psalm 119:11, the psalmist states, "I have hidden your word in my heart that I might not sin against you." Throughout your day, take small sections of this verse and savor them slowly: I have + hidden + your word + in + my heart + that I might not + sin against you.

Exercise:

1. Pick up your Bible and pray. Thank God for the gift you hold in your hands. Ask the Holy Spirit to teach you and lead you into truth.

2. Review your research and study notes from chapters 22 and 23.

3. Picture Jesus addressing the disciples after He washed their feet, predicted Judas's betrayal, and foretold Peter's denial. What emotions could the disciples have experienced as they listened to Jesus' words?

4. Read John 14 quietly and carefully in one sitting with these questions in mind:

   • Attempt to place yourself in the scene with the Eleven. What might Jesus' words have meant to them then?

   • Three disciples who are rarely quoted in the Gospels speak in this chapter. Who were they and what did they ask?

   • Jesus is preparing His disciples for His departure. What does Jesus emphasize in this time of transition for the disciples?

5. Highlight any sentences that might have been a mystery to the Eleven until after Jesus' resurrection. Star any sentences that remain a mystery to you almost two thousand years later.

6. Now shift from "What did it mean to them then?" to "What does this mean to us now?" Place an asterisk by the principles and truths that are timeless. Then think of an area in which your heart is troubled (v. 1). What do these timeless truths mean to you today?

7. Finally, "extract the essence" of a verse by a method popularized by seventeenth-century writer Jeanne Guyon.[17]

   • In John 14, select one phrase that seems especially meaningful to you in this moment.

   • Quiet your heart and savor each word slowly in prayer. Like a fabulous chunk of chocolate, allow each word to be tasted and treasured in your mind.

   • Often this process ushers us into a sweet awareness of God's presence. Rest there, whispering truths of God's character as a love offering.

WHEN THE WORD IS HEARD AND HEEDED

If someone based their views, choices, and values on a source that you perceived to be inaccurate at best and misleading at worst, they would not gain ground with you by quoting that source. I understand. For me as an atheist, when people referred to the Bible, they gained about as much ground as if they had referenced Jiminy Cricket, Pinocchio's fairy-tale conscience. In other words, they lost ground every time they said, "It is written . . ."

When Christian friends gave me little Bibles, I stacked them in the recesses of my bathroom since culturally I could not bring myself to throw a gift away. Every once in a while (only after I had read and reread the most current issue of *National Geographic*, the back of my shampoo bottle, and the bottom of the Kleenex box), out of sheer boredom I would reach for one of those little books.

Flipping through the onionskin pages, I scanned the tiny King James print and saw *nothing*. Not that the pages were blank. The very words were insubstantial to me. Letter after letter and line upon line passed through my eye gate, ran into my mind, and slid off.

"What nonsense," I would moan and put the gift aside.

However, when God suddenly *was*, I ached for a Bible. I thirsted for one like I thirsted for water. When I held one—how can I say this?—it was *alive*. I could not hear it or read it fast enough. So I read and read, not to learn what I was supposed to do or what I was supposed to believe, but to discover Who had interrupted my existence. Did I understand all of it? No. But I was not reading to teach, I was reading because I had to hear—I had to experience—the *Voice*.[1]

I fell in love with the Word because the Voice incarnate captivated me. The author of Psalm 119 was devoted to the Voice one thousand years before Jesus walked the earth.

In the last chapter, we considered the psalmist's commitment to God's Word. Here, we will examine what God's voice can accomplish in a heart that listens and obeys. Once again, the verses are listed in order of frequency. And once again, I invite you to avoid scanning and slowly read each verse, asking a question: "What would change in my relationship with God's Word if I believed that this were true?"

The Word heard and heeded

- Provides perspective in times of suffering (four times)[2]
- Preserves our lives (two times)[3]
- Grants us understanding to hate every wrong path (two times)[4]
- Makes it possible for us to walk in God's ways (v. 3)
- Keeps the path of the young pure (v. 9)
- Trains us not to sin against God (v. 11)
- Is a counselor (v. 24)
- Strengthens us (v. 28)
- Enables us to find delight (v. 35)
- Empowers us to walk about in freedom (v. 45)
- Comforts us (v. 52)
- Gives us a theme song (v. 54)
- Prevents us from going astray (v. 67)
- Makes us wiser than our enemies (v. 98)
- Gifts us with more insight than teachers (v. 99)
- Bestows on us more understanding than elders (v. 100)

- Is how God teaches us (v. 102)
- Is a lamp to our feet and a light to our path (v. 105)
- Fills our hearts with joy (v. 111)
- Offers light and understanding to the simple (v. 130)
- Strengthens us so that sin will not rule over us (v. 133)
- Imparts great peace (v. 165)
- Delivers us from stumbling (v. 165)

Incredible.

What could the Word heard and heeded do in a nation? A community? A business? A family? One heart? Imagine what could happen if we heeded the counsel of Oswald Chambers, who said, "Never compromise with those who water down the word of God to human experience, instead of allowing God to lift up our experience to His Word."[5]

OUR FREQUENT DAILY PRAYERS	WHEN THE WORD IS HEARD AND HEEDED, IT . . .
Teach me Your ways.	Makes it possible for us to walk in God's ways
I want to be pure.	Keeps the path of the young pure
Help me not sin.	Trains us not to sin against God
Lead me.	Is a counselor
Save me.	Preserves our lives
Strengthen me.	Strengthens us
Fill me with Your joy.	Enables us to find delight
Free me.	Empowers us to walk about in freedom
Comfort me.	Comforts us
Guide me.	Gives us a theme song

OUR FREQUENT DAILY PRAYERS	WHEN THE WORD IS HEARD AND HEEDED, IT . . .
Guard me.	Prevents us from going astray
Why?	Provides perspective in times of suffering
I need wisdom!	Makes us wiser than our enemies
Grant me insight.	Gifts us with more insight than teachers
Give me understanding.	Bestows on us more understanding than elders
Teach me.	Is how God teaches us
May I hate what You hate.	Grants us understanding to hate every wrong path
Show me Your path.	Is a lamp to our feet and a light to our path
Fill me with joy.	Fills our hearts with joy
Speak to me.	Offers light and understanding to the simple
May sin not rule over me.	Strengthens us so that sin will not rule over us
Give me peace.	Imparts great peace
Deliver me from evil.	Delivers us from stumbling

Allow me to reformat the psalmist's stunning list alongside our most common prayers:

Such is the power of God's glorious voice! No wonder the psalmist declared, "My heart is set on keeping your decrees to the very end" (Psalm 119:112).

❚❚ GUIDED RESPONSE

Thought Focus:

Discipline your heart to pause after prayers (like those listed above) and ask God to direct you to His Word for answers, strength, wisdom, and protection. For example, *My God, I desperately need peace of mind. Lead me to Your Word!* Then simply wait a minute to give opportunity for God's Spirit to bring a passage or verse to your mind to read or savor.

Exercise:

Note: As we continue our study of John 14–17, many of the directions below will be familiar from the last chapter's exercise. This is intentional. My hope is that repetition will assist us in establishing a rhythm of study.

1. Pick up your Bible and pray. Thank God for the gift you hold in your hands. Ask the Holy Spirit to teach you and lead you into truth.
2. Review your research and study notes from chapters 22, 23, and 24.
3. Read John 15 and 16 quietly and carefully in one sitting with these thoughts in mind:
   - Attempt to place yourself in the scene with the Eleven. What might Jesus' words have meant to them then?
   - Remember that Jesus is preparing His disciples for His departure. Make a list of what Jesus tells the disciples to expect in the future.
   - Create a written collage of the words, descriptors, and images that Jesus uses to describe Himself.
   - Create a written collage of the words, descriptors, and images that Jesus uses to describe the Holy Spirit.
   - List any clear commands Jesus gives to His disciples.

4. Highlight sentences that might have been a mystery to the Eleven until after Jesus' resurrection. Take note of sentences that remain a mystery to you almost two thousand years later.

5. Now transition from "What did it mean to them then?" to "What does this mean to us now?"

   - In 16:1, Jesus explains, "All this I have told you so that you will not fall away." Prayerfully identify an area in which you are vulnerable to straying in thought or deed.

   - Consider what meaning the observations you made in question 3 may have for you in this area of weakness.

A REQUEST FOR MORE

A young woman brought home a man who wanted to date her so that we could meet him. After dinner, I asked a sequence of rather tame questions like, "Why are you dating our beloved Rebekkah? When did you first notice her? What is it about her that you are drawn to? What are your intentions toward her?" With wide eyes, Gabe looked for support from Barry, who smiled and said, "I was going to bring a shotgun, but I brought my wife instead."

Gabe took a deep breath, collected his thoughts, and then began to talk sincerely and substantially about Rebekkah and his respect for her. No spin. No fluff. No flattery. He had studied her for months and described her strength, faith, and beauty with accuracy and admiration.

My point is this: it is easy to talk about what we admire, study, and love. The anonymous pen of Psalm 119 clearly admired, studied, and loved God's Word. As we have already seen, this psalmist-mentor talked to God about his commitment to God's Word (what the Word is) and about his belief in the power of God's Word (what the Word does). And he still had more to say! The third component of his psalm was to scripture-pray to God for an *even greater* relationship with His Word.

Psalm 119 is punctuated with many prayer requests, most of which are supported by God's promises. The psalmist asked God to strengthen him according to God's Word, to sustain him according to God's promise, and to preserve his life according to God's laws, promises, and Word.[1]

Present among his petitions, however, is a unique set of prayer requests expressly *about* God's Word.

> As a leader, the psalmist had access to the Word.
> Literate, he could read the Word.
> Educated, he could study the Word.
> Skilled, he could write about the Word.
> Yet this lover of the Word ached for *more*.

In these eighteen Word-focused prayers, I see four broad themes as listed below. Read the psalmist's three-thousand-year-old requests thoughtfully and then join me in a scripture-prayer from each theme.

GOD, OPEN MY SPIRITUAL EYES.

VERSE	SCRIPTURE
18	Open my eyes that I may see wonderful things in your law.
19	I am a stranger on earth; do not hide your commands from me.
43	Never take your word of truth from my mouth, for I have put my hope in your laws.

> *My God, You are my true home, and I am a stranger on this earth.*
> *Your Word is my life-source.*
> *May all that You have spoken remain in me.*
> *May I speak Your truth all my days.*
> *Oh God, open my spiritual eyes.*
> *May I always live in awe and wonder of Your Word.*

GOD, BE MY TEACHER.

VERSE	SCRIPTURE
26	I gave an account of my ways and you answered me; teach me your decrees.
64	The earth is filled with your love, LORD; teach me your decrees.
68	You are good, and what you do is good; teach me your decrees.
108	Accept, LORD, the willing praise of my mouth, and teach me your laws.
124	Deal with your servant according to your love and teach me your decrees.
135	Make your face shine on your servant and teach me your decrees.

My God, You are loving and Your ways are good.
You hear and answer me, so I ask this of You: Be my teacher.
Instruct me personally by Your Holy Spirit.
I long to be God-taught, not self-taught.
Shine on me as Your servant.
O Lord of love, mentor my mind.

GOD, GIVE ME UNDERSTANDING.

VERSE	SCRIPTURE
27	Cause me to understand the way of your precepts, that I may meditate on your wonderful deeds.
34	Give me understanding, so that I may keep your law and obey it with all my heart.
73	Your hands made me and formed me; give me understanding to learn your commands.
125	I am your servant; give me discernment that I may understand your statutes.
169	Give me understanding according to your word.

My God, You created me.
My mind is God-formed.

My spirit is God-breathed.
Grant me a discerning mind to comprehend Your Word.
Inspire my spirit to learn and obey Your commands.
I am Your servant: gift me with insight.
Beyond seeing and hearing, inspire my understanding and
wonder of Your Word.

GOD, DIRECT MY RESPONSE.

VERSE	SCRIPTURE
33	Teach me, LORD, the way of your decrees, that I may follow it to the end.
35	Direct me in the path of your commands.
36	Turn my heart toward your statutes and not toward selfish gain.
133	Direct my footsteps according to your word; let no sin rule over me.

God, empower me to be a doer of the Word and not a
hearer only.
You have opened my spiritual eyes.
You have become my teacher.
You have granted me understanding.
Now help me to live according to Your truth.
May Your Word in my heart determine the direction for
my life.
May Your truth in my spirit be reflected in the path taken
by my feet.
By Your presence, lean me always toward Your ways until
the day I touch Your face.

⊪ GUIDED RESPONSE

Thought Focus:
Write down any sentences or phrases that especially stand out to

you from these scripture-prayers. Place these prayers within sight and direct them to God whenever you see them. May God increase our hunger and respect for His life-giving Word.

Exercise:

1. Pick up your Bible and pray. Thank God for the gift you hold in your hands. Ask the Holy Spirit to teach you and lead you into truth.
2. Briefly review your study notes from chapters 22–25. In particular, refresh your memory of what occurs immediately following John 17 (see chapter 22, exercise 3).
3. Read John 17 aloud in one sitting.
   - Attempt to place yourself in the scene with the Eleven. After listening to Jesus' words recorded in John 14–16, what might it have felt like to hear Jesus pray in John 17?
   - Take note of any parts of Jesus' prayer that seem to directly address themes He discussed in John 14–16.
   - Make a list of Jesus' personal prayer requests to Father God.
   - What could the listening disciples have learned about Jesus from His prayer?
4. Highlight sentences that might have been a mystery to the Eleven until after Jesus' resurrection. Take note of sentences that remain a mystery to you almost two thousand years later.
5. Now transition from "What did it mean to them then?" to "What does this mean to us now?" Underline any sentences that are especially encouraging for you today.
6. As you place a comma in your study of John 14–17, summarize the principles from your study that have resonated most deeply in your spirit.

DISCOVERING GOD-PRINTS

> And now for your blunders . . . [you] allowed the patient to read a book he really enjoyed . . . [and] walk down to the old mill and have tea there—a walk through country he really likes, and taken alone. In other words, you allowed him two real positive Pleasures. Were you so ignorant as not to see the danger of this? The characteristic of Pains and Pleasures is that they are unmistakably real, and therefore, as far as they go, give the man who feels them a touchstone of reality.[1]
>
> —C. S. LEWIS, *THE SCREWTAPE LETTERS: WITH SCREWTAPE PROPOSES A TOAST*

WHAT YOU WILL NEED FOR THE EXERCISES

- ✔ A notepad *or* journal
- ✔ A Bible
- ✔ Three or four discerning friends

SPLOSHY

On the day that Jesus interrupted my atheistic worldview, His presence was pervasive.

I felt like a sponge.

Until that moment, I thought dry and stiff was normal and even strong. But in that flood of God's presence, my soul instinctively began to soak up God's reality.

The presence kept pouring over me, and by the time I left that little church, it seemed that every step I took left a watermark. I could almost hear the fresh, sploshy sounds: one step with Jesus, two steps with Jesus, one hour with Jesus, two hours with Jesus . . .

Hopefully, I have been leaving sploshy prints ever since that day.

For those of you who have already checked, you are correct: *sploshy* is not in the dictionary. But you know what it means. *Sploshy* captures the sound, the weight, and the evidence of something that is saturated.

For a sponge, *sploshy* is the evidence of fullness. For a soul, *sploshy* is the overflow of presence.

That initial encounter with Jesus gave me insight into how I was designed to soak up God: sploshy commenced for me in the midst of corporate worship. Whether your first steps in Jesus were distinct moments still lit with wonder, a warm but vague memory, or a series of conscious—but not sensory rich—choices, your soul[1] experienced home in a way that your mind may always struggle to articulate.

Because you have been custom-created to know God, no origin story can nullify that design. No sin can void that code. No wound can banish that blueprint. Pain and shame may bury that design in shadows, but nothing can erase God's fingerprints from your soul.

God really did design you to know Him personally. Maturity in Christ is not doing more, it is discovering more about Who He is and how He has crafted you to know Him and make Him known.

For me, a few activities and disciplines have consistently saturated my soul with God's presence:

- Reading biographies of faithful Jesus-followers
- Staring at bare (but not barren) trees in winter[2]
- Walking along un-manicured, woody paths
- Playing a piano in an empty room
- Journaling my prayers to God
- Sitting near running streams
- Listening to classical music
- Painting to worship songs
- Studying the Scriptures
- Writing by candlelight
- Savoring silence

Once discovered, I actively pursue and protect these practices because they are reflective of how God architected me to know Him. Do I experience all these options every day? No. But with intentionality I shape each day with the opportunity to experience at least one. Today, for example, I took a walk in our country land, and now I am writing by a lit candle. Each willful choice to know and nourish my God-print feels like a love letter to my Creator. They are small ways that I can whisper, "I love You."

We will explore more of this God-print concept in the coming chapters, but for now consider two abstract but critical questions:

How has God architected you to know Him?

How, when, and where does your spirit feel *sploshy*?

ⅠⅠ GUIDED RESPONSE

The five chapters of movement seven focus on discovering, celebrating, and nurturing our God-prints.

Collectively, we reflect God's infinite creativity.

Individually, we reflect God's profound personalization.

We all bear His fingerprints.

Look at your hands. Touch your face. Wiggle your toes. If a spiritual private investigator dusted you, he would find God's unique fingerprints in every pore.

Thought Focus:

Think back over the last twenty-four hours and identify the motivations that characterized your leadership at work, in the church, or at home.

Values	Obligation	Desire for order
Stress	Commitment	Faith
Love	Fear	Jealousy
Impatience	God's Presence	Anger
Servanthood	Shame	Compassion
Hope	Insecurity	Other

Which relationships are benefiting most from your increasingly *sploshy* soul?

Exercise:

1. Slowly and carefully consider this sentence penned by King David. Meditate on it word by word. Journal your thoughts or reflections.

> For you created my inmost being;
>> you knit me together in my mother's womb.
>
> (Psalm 139:13)

2. Recall contexts, experiences, and places in which your spirit seemed to soak up God's presence. Perhaps a solitary run in the early morning? A monthly time with colleagues at the coffee shop? A conference? Your violin? That park? Fishing at dawn? Meetings with a mentor?
3. Stretch as far back as you can in your memory to identify these experiences and record them in your journal or notepad.
4. Take special note of any commonalities. For example, do they often involve nature? Art? Working with your hands? Certain seasons? Mornings? Specific relationships?

A WALL AND A DOOR

How has God architected you to know Him? This question could be life giving.

Over the last decades as a mentor and spiritual director, I have stared into the eyes of numerous earnest souls who drew a complete blank when faced with some version of this question.

Two groups in particular consistently respond to the question with a "could you please rephrase the interrogative" lost look: passionate visionaries and diligent church workers.

Both groups can easily answer other questions including, "What are your giftings? How has God called you to serve? How are you making a difference?"

Both groups know how to give, how to lead, how to help, how to initiate, how to follow through.

And both groups are vulnerable to waking up one day and feeling spent, exhausted, and perhaps even used.

Passionate visionaries know they are uniquely made, but they can easily confuse experiencing God for being intimate with God. The blush of a dream pursued, the rush of a dream fulfilled. Adrenaline, mistaken for devotion, can propel them from vision to vision.

Diligent church workers and hard-working volunteers sometimes describe their experience of God's presence as event related: this service, that moment, this place, and that preacher. Though unspeakably grateful for such memories, they rarely dare to take them personally and are "just blessed" to have been in the right place at the right time when God was "pouring out His presence."

So onward both groups go year after year and decade upon decade, for the love of God and His people: highly productive, servant hearted, continually volunteering and assisting and giving and going . . . until one day when they hit a wall.

And from their parched lips, we may hear these whispers:

"It's endless. I'm always behind. I can't do it anymore."
"I'm tired of being the cheerleader. Reality rarely measures up to my dreams."
"I don't feel God. I go through the motions. I pray, but it's like I'm just talking to myself."

The wall—though cold to the touch—is actually a gift. Within the wall is a door. What seems like an end is a glorious invitation to discover a new dimension of living.

God never wanted to use us.
He has always longed to love us.

Our Creator has waited for us to see and celebrate His customized fingerprints in our unique DNA. He aches for our service to flow not from passion or responsibility alone, but from *fullness* as we live each moment with Him.

So let us slow, let us seek, and let us find how God has uniquely designed us to know Him, to love Him, and to be loved by Him in every breath.

❚❚ GUIDED RESPONSE

Thought Focus:

In the chapter reading, underline any familiarities you may have noticed with the spiritual profile of a "passionate visionary" or "diligent church worker." Whether the page remains untouched or every other sentence is underlined, ask God to help you understand how He architected you to know Him.

Exercise:

1. Slowly and carefully consider the next sentence penned by King David. Meditate on it word by word. Journal your thoughts or reflections.

   > I praise you because I am fearfully and wonderfully made;
   >   your works are wonderful,
   > I know that full well. (Psalm 139:14)

2. Take action from the last chapter's discoveries. In the next few days, make room for one of the experiences you identified. For example,
   - Purchase a few painting supplies.
   - Go to sleep early to wake up in time for that early prayer meeting.
   - Place your running gear right by your bed and welcome the new day running and talking with Jesus.
   - Message that accountability friend.
   - Switch off all media, fill your favorite cup with your favorite coffee, and savor a spiritual biography.

3. Afterward, dream with God. What might the two of you add, delete, or edit next time to continue to align your soul with how He designed you to know Him in every breath?

OUR ORIGINAL ARTIST

"Every piece has a story," my artist friend explained. "This painting speaks of a spiritual journey. That piece was birthed from the joys and aches of parenthood. They are all intensely personal."[1]

Intensely personal, she said. Every stroke of her brush flowed from an idea, feeling, longing, or message. Her art is an expression of herself.

What a moving reflection of our original Artist.

Join me in imagining a heavenly conversation . . .

Almighty, the look on Your face is intriguing. I see intensity and joy, creativity and love. May I inquire: What are You doing?

Ah, yes, My angelic friend, I am creating Esther Adanna. Her earthly father is from Nigeria, and her mother is of Persian descent. I'm adding a hint of green to her deep brown eyes and framing her cheekbones with rich, thick hair curled tightly around her full face. And her nimble hands—oh, the first time she holds a violin, what a day that will be! She will sense Me when she plays, though she may not yet know My name.

I see, Lord! Is this an image of what she will look like? Thank You, Lord, but what of her legs? One seems much shorter than the other. Do You plan to heal her to reveal Yourself?

Such a gift, friend, would not be necessary in heaven. But the gift is needed on earth.

Gift? You mean the gift of her healing?

No, the gift of her weakness will turn her from certain paths and tenderize her spirit. I have placed within her a great capacity for compassion. She will have eyes to see the forgotten. There, too, she will sense Me. I have also imprinted on her My love for the sciences so she will be sensitive to the wonder of My creation.

Lord, when You sighed deeply just now, was that breath for Esther Adanna?

Yes, her life has just begun! For now, only you and I know of her existence. Others will join us soon. Over the years, some will applaud her life and some will scar her life. But My eyes alone will never, ever leave or forsake her.

Amazing. And what are Your plans for her?

My plans? I plan to love her. I plan for her to awaken to Me and the true meaning of her name.[2] I plan to sing to her on earth and become her life-song. I plan to touch others through the hands I designed.

And then one day My own hand will touch Esther Adanna. Her days will number eighty-nine years. One spring morning I will call My daughter home. Then I will hold her curly head in My hands and take her on a tour of the stars that she loves. We will listen to the angels sing and play the violin together. And in heaven, though whole, she will lean upon Me because her gift will have taught her to lean.

So, until then, Esther Adanna, My sweet daughter, grow and know that I am God.

GUIDED RESPONSE

Thought Focus:

Personalize Esther Adanna's story by inserting your name, heritage, weaknesses, and interests into the dialogue above. Ponder the presence of God's fingerprints on your bones, skin, and longings.

Exercise:

1. Slowly and carefully consider the next sentence penned by King David. Meditate on it word by word and journal your reflections.

   My frame was not hidden from you
   when I was made in the secret place,
   when I was woven together in the depths of the earth.
   (Psalm 139:15)

2. Contact three or four friends who consistently model spiritual depth and ask them for ten to fifteen minutes of time by phone, e-mail, or in person. Briefly update them on your Sacred Slow journey and share the reading from chapter 27 with them on the concept of living sploshy.
3. Ask them some version of the following: "Knowing me, if you could design a context in which I would spiritually thrive—live saturated with God's presence—what would it look like? What would be present? Absent? What would I do? Not do?"
   - For example, if my husband asked me this question, my reply would be: "I would design a context with a hobby farm, an organic garden, prayer-walking trails through the woods, a room filled with stringed instruments, another room filled with books and a fabulous recliner, and an open invitation for others to visit and learn God's

ways from you. A CPA would do all the finances, and you would never have to respond to another e-mail or fill out even one more report. You would have the space to meet face-to-face with everyone. The cupboards would be filled with organic chai, and every room would have a fireplace. You would have a lifetime membership to your favorite golf course, a dream set of clubs, a large John Deere tractor with a generous assortment of attachments to dig and mow to your heart's content, and a serious chain saw that does not break down after a hard day's work. And your only focus would be loving God, loving family, intercession, mentoring, growing goodness from God's earth, and tending your soul."

- From this, you can see that my husband's spirit is best tended in outside walks and talks with Jesus, writing and playing worship songs, the absence of administrative responsibilities, the presence of shoulder-to-shoulder relationships, gardening, intercession, thick family time, and morning rounds of golf (which is always therapeutic—really, you should try it).

4. Take careful notes of your friends' responses and pay special attention to repeated themes.

5. Next, draft a personal God-print statement: "God has created me in such a way that I thrive when_____ are present and _____ are absent. My spirit soaks up His presence through _____ and _____. Activities that drain that reserve are _____ and _____. So a dream day for my spirit would be _____."

- Obviously, like my husband, you probably cannot dismiss all the drains and focus exclusively on the gains. However, these exercises can influence how you spend your resources and how you are shaping your future.

- For example, featured prominently in Barry's office is his collection of stringed instruments. In this season, he rarely can get lost in writing music, but the nearness of these small treasures waters his spirit in the midst of the administrative tasks that await him each day.

6. Based on your friends' insights, what should you guard and nurture for the sake of your soul? In the future, would it be spiritually beneficial to minimize, delegate, or phase out certain tasks or responsibilities?

AN INTERNAL AIR FRESHENER

"What are you thankful for today?" we prompt our children as we drive into town.

This is a question they expect. Every day we buckle up, sing a prayer of protection, and then express gratitude for at least one thing. The family tradition grows gratitude, a discipline that safeguards spiritual intimacy.

Spiritual intimacy? Yes. Gratitude is an internal air freshener. As a discipline, gratitude aggressively diffuses a master saboteur of relationships: negativity.

Allow me to illustrate from the life of Ella.

I was grafted into Ella's family through marriage. Barry deeply loved his grandmother, and I quickly understood why. Ella walked with God. Although her heartaches were many, they formed her but did not define her. Gratitude made the difference.

Aging seems to be its own wilderness—a physical desert where weakness is the norm and loss is a constant companion. Yet as Ella's body diminished, her spirit swelled. Surely this takes work. Pain does not of its own accord grow intimacy. I watched carefully to discern the work Ella had chosen.

Ella loved crafts and nature, especially gardening and bird watching. No doubt these activities contributed to a sploshy spirit in years gone by, but, one by one, such options thinned. Ella transitioned from working the garden, to watching others work the garden, to not even being able to see the garden.

One particular day is etched in my memory. My son, Jonathan, was around three years old when the two of us were with Grandma Ella in her living room. She sat in her chair facing the window, and Jonathan played on the carpet. I went to the kitchen for a moment and returned to find tears trickling down Ella's face.

"Grandma, did something happen? Did something startle you?" I asked.

"No," she said with a tender voice. "No, dear. I'm just so grateful to God."

I touched her thin, silky hand and paused to consider the losses she knew: loved ones, health, mobility, sight.

Then she continued, "When Jonathan stands in front of the window, I can see his shadow!"

She was grateful.
She was grateful to see shadows.

Such is the fruit of gratitude as a discipline. Decade upon decade, gratitude sweetened and expanded Ella's spirit even when the pain of life soured her health and shrunk her world.

This discipline of gratitude is a guardian of intimacy because it trains us to discern God's presence in every season.

It is one thing for gratitude to occasionally decorate our lives in moments of joy. It is another thing for gratitude to be a daily exercise.

The former is natural.
The latter is a choice.
And the latter refreshes our God-prints.

❚❚ GUIDED RESPONSE

Thought Focus:

Contemplate the life and choices of an aging friend or relative whose spirit seems to become sweeter with every passing year.

Exercise:

1. Slowly and carefully consider the following verses penned by King David. Meditate on them word by word, journaling your reflections.

   > I was woven together in the depths of the earth.
   > Your eyes saw my unformed body. (Psalm 139:15–16)

2. In the last chapter, you drafted a personal God-print statement summarizing your current understanding of how God designed you to spiritually thrive. Reread that statement and asterisk any activity that may be affected by the passing of time. Reflecting on Ella's life was motivational for me. While I *can* walk outside, I need to walk outside. While I *can* play the piano, I need to play the piano. More options to respond to my God-print are available today than may be accessible in coming decades.

3. Is gratitude an established discipline or an occasional decoration in your life? Creatively consider how to further cultivate this guardian of spiritual intimacy. For example:
   - Journal one point of gratitude daily.
   - Start a gratitude journal.
   - Identify a normal moment each day such as a meal or travel time to verbalize specific points of gratitude.

- Make a reminder note and place it in a space where you are vulnerable to negativity, like on a computer or in a bathroom.
- Choose to make your last thought at night, *Thank You, God, for . . .*

THE POSITIVE POWER
OF PURE PLEASURE

One sentence in *Chariots of Fire* always arrests me: "I believe that God made me for a purpose. But He also made me fast, and when I run, I feel His pleasure."[1]

Eric Liddell's words reveal a soul that discovered and nurtured its God-print.

China was God's choice of geographic bookends for Eric's forty-three years on earth.[2] Liddell was born there in 1902 and died there in 1945. In between, he grew up in a boarding school in England, received a science degree from the University of Edinburgh, won a gold medal at the 1924 Olympics, and in 1925 returned to China as a missionary.

From his feats as Scotland's most famous runner to his final years of compassionate service in an internment camp, Liddell's sploshy spirit affected all who met him. Competitors and fellow prisoners knew they were in the presence of a man who walked, and ran, with God.

Though reportedly not pretty, Eric Liddell's running style was powerful. Perhaps his run—head back, mouth open—resembled King David's dance. Discovering God's pleasure is simply too precious to modify for the sake of onlookers.

Perhaps our run is also less than pretty and our painting less than professional. Perhaps "making a joyful noise" for us is not figurative and gardening is mostly therapeutic.

Excellence does not authenticate our God-prints.

So turn on the worship music and dance to your heart's content. Fish when nothing is biting. Play the piano like no one is listening. Camp when only mosquitoes will thank you. Write without editing. Run—as Liddell did—for an audience of One.

Nurturing our God-prints enables us to spiritually thrive even when the scenery changes.

In his first decades, Liddell ran on country paths and Olympic tracks with speed, skill, and strength:

> He felt God's pleasure,
>> the world celebrated,
>>> heaven smiled, and
>>>> hell was annoyed.

In his last decades, Liddell served selflessly while a brain tumor painfully shaved off the edges of his life:

> He knew God's presence,
>> the world wondered why he had not stayed home,
>>> heaven wept with wonder, and
>>>> hell trembled.

The kingdom of darkness shudders when confronted by a soul that discovers, nurtures, celebrates, and is seasoned in the day of pain by its God-prints.

⏸ GUIDED RESPONSE

In this seventh movement, we have with intentionality explored old and new means that reflect how God personally architected us to spiritually thrive. We now conclude this God-print emphasis of *The Sacred Slow* with celebration.

Thought Focus:

Watch *Chariots of Fire* or read an article about an Olympian or professional athlete whose faith inspires their game. Then attempt to fill in the blank of Liddell's quote for yourself: When I _____, I feel God's pleasure.

Exercise:

Liddell ran and David danced. When David's wife rebuked him for dancing in the streets, he replied, "I will celebrate before the LORD. I will become even more undignified than this, and I will be humiliated in my own eyes. But by these slave girls you spoke of, I will be held in honor" (2 Samuel 6:21–22). Celebration inspired David's dance. A close cousin of gratitude, celebration turns our gaze upward.

1. Slowly and carefully consider the next sentence from King David. Meditate on it word by word, journaling your reflections.

   All the days ordained for me were written in your book before one of them came to be. (Psalm 139:16)

2. Set aside ten minutes of private space and open your Bible to Psalms 147–150.

3. Select and read aloud one of these psalms in a way that honors the psalm's author.

4. Then, in a journal and with your voice, complete at least a dozen variations of "God, in Your presence, I celebrate _____."

5. Pay attention to any desires or longings this exercise stirs within you like shouting, running, singing, or serving. They may be reflective of your God-print.

THE DISCIPLINE OF RESTRAINT

> What we *are* is of much more use to God and our fellows than what we *do*.
> Be absolutely His![1]
>
> —Oswald Chambers, *Oswald Chambers: Abandoned to God*

WHAT YOU WILL NEED FOR THE EXERCISES

✔ A Bible
✔ A notepad *or* journal
✔ Space to walk near nature
✔ A friend

CAN ≠ SHOULD

Go where people can see you.
Become a public figure.
Show yourself to the world.

Though such sentences sound like publicity pushes from an affirming agent or enthusiastic marketer, this advice is actually ancient:

> Jesus' brothers said to him, "Leave Galilee and go to Judea, so that your disciples there may see the works you do. No one who wants to become a public figure acts in secret. Since you are doing these things, show yourself to the world." For even his own brothers did not believe in him.
>
> Therefore Jesus told them, "My time is not yet here; for you any time will do." (John 7:3–6)

With their eyebrows raised in familial skepticism, Jesus' brothers basically said, "What's up with you? Why are you holding back? If you want to change the world, you need to make a name for yourself."

The exchange is revealing of the fundamentally different equations influencing their lives.

For the brothers:

can = should
can dictated timing

For Jesus:

can ≠ should
can submitted to timing

And for us?

This discipline of restraint that Jesus exemplifies is as mysterious to us as it was to Jesus' brothers, which implies that human nature in general—not just certain cultures in particular—struggles to grasp the value of *holding back* when one is able to *push forward*.

We normally diagnose holding back as a manifestation of fear. In Jesus, however, we see that holding back can also be a manifestation of love. In the poetic words of Henry David Thoreau, "If a man does not keep pace with his companions, perhaps it is because he hears a different drummer. Let him step to the music which he hears, however measured or far away."[1] The discipline of restraint hears and heeds the sound of a different Drummer.

> Very truly I tell you, the Son can do nothing by himself; he can do only what he sees his Father doing, because whatever the Father does the Son also does. (John 5:19)

> I love the Father and do exactly what my Father has commanded me. (John 14:31)

Though a cousin of humility, the discipline of restraint is not related to *timidity*.

Though a friend of patience, the discipline of restraint is not a form of *hesitation*.

Timidity is fear driven.

Hesitation is doubt driven.

Restraint is obedience inspired.

As we commence our five-chapter focus on this somewhat counterintuitive discipline, consider this distinction:

> Jesus' brothers wanted Him to *push ahead*.
> But Jesus chose to live *led*.

❚❚ GUIDED RESPONSE

Thought Focus:

Meditate on the restraint exemplified in Jesus' words to His brothers: "My time is not yet here; for you any time will do" (John 7:6).

Exercise:

fast *verb*

1: to abstain from food

2: to eat sparingly or abstain from some foods[2]

1. Explore the most familiar form of the discipline of restraint: fasting. Though a rich multitude of fasting options and purposes exist, I invite you to join me in what some call the Bridegroom Fast:

   The purpose of the Bridegroom fast goes even beyond yearning for Jesus' return—it is the yearning to experience His presence now. In the midst of the delay, the waiting between His first and second coming, God allows us to experience a measure of His presence. He has sent the Holy Spirit so we can encounter His presence and love in measure even now. The Bridegroom fast enlarges our hearts to experience that divine love and presence now.[3]

2. Read the following passage slowly:

> Then John's disciples came and asked him, "How is it that we and the Pharisees fast often, but your disciples do not fast?"
>
> Jesus answered, "How can the guests of the bridegroom mourn while he is with them? The time will come when the bridegroom will be taken from them; then they will fast." (Matthew 9:14–15)

3. Prayerfully plan a fast:
   - Choose a fasting option that is appropriate as opposed to strenuous. Take into account personal medical conditions and energy requirements. For example, you may choose to fast meat, sugar, or caffeine. Though the fast should be a denial of something you normally would eat or drink, the goal is not asceticism.
   - Select a time period for your Bridegroom Fast, such as an afternoon or a day.
   - Be mindful of the place in which you will fast. Prepare yourself in advance for how to adjust or flex if your fast extends into office hours or family activities.
4. Begin your fast with a simple prayer such as, *Jesus, I long for You*. Then, during your fast, meditate on one of the following passages:

> They came to John and said to him, "Rabbi, that man who was with you on the other side of the Jordan— the one you testified about—look, he is baptizing, and everyone is going to him."
>
> To this John replied, "A person can receive only what is given them from heaven. You yourselves can testify that I said, 'I am not the Messiah but am sent ahead of him.'

The bride belongs to the bridegroom. The friend who attends the bridegroom waits and listens for him, and is full of joy when he hears the bridegroom's voice. That joy is mine, and it is now complete. He must become greater; I must become less." (John 3:26–30)

"Look, I am coming soon! My reward is with me, and I will give to each person according to what they have done. I am the Alpha and the Omega, the First and the Last, the Beginning and the End. . . .

"I, Jesus, have sent my angel to give you this testimony for the churches. I am the Root and the Offspring of David, and the bright Morning Star." The Spirit and the bride say, "Come!" And let the one who hears say, "Come!" Let the one who is thirsty come; and let the one who wishes take the free gift of the water of life. (Revelation 22:12–13, 17)

5. Journal any thoughts you have during this experience.

LIVING *LED*

Jesus' example makes it clear that living *led* is not a passive default for souls who lack either the strength to direct or the passion to dream.

Jesus' *led* was muscular and authoritative.
Such is the discipline of restraint.

Restraint is volitional. Synonyms for restraint include *self-control, command, self-possession, self-discipline,* and *moderation.*

Most often we think of restraint as a choice to *not* do something we would later regret, e.g., "I wanted to say something but I was too angry to trust myself, so I kept my mouth shut." Or, "He was asking for a fight, but I refused to be baited." We define *restraint* as emotional control in difficult contexts.

In Jesus, however, we witness an even deeper dimension of restraint. Not only did Jesus control His emotions, Jesus submitted His strengths. Jesus trained His giftings and abilities to follow the lead of His Father's will and timing.

Jesus did not perform miracles on demand.
Jesus did not travel every time a door opened.
Jesus did not heal every time there was a need.
Jesus did not lead every time the people looked to Him.
Jesus did not preach every time multitudes gathered.

To live *led* is to live inspired by Another, as opposed to inspired by opportunity.

That dimension of restraint acknowledges that we are stewards (not owners) of the giftings and strengths God has entrusted to us.

That dimension of restraint floods every moment with a thick, God-size purpose.

That dimension of restraint grows within us a glorious immunity to circumstance and opinion.

> Scenery did not cue Jesus.
> Crowds could not woo Jesus.
> Obscurity did not discourage Jesus.
> Fame did not distract Jesus.

Thank God.

When a yes is inspired by God's timing and spoken in submission to God's will, the servant is guarded and the Giver is glorified.

 # GUIDED RESPONSE

Thought Focus:

Consider the contrast of a yes that is inspired by opportunity and a yes that is inspired by God. What differences (if any) might be visible to onlookers? What differences (if any) might you discern within yourself?

Exercise:

1. Physically, strength training involves intentional cycles of exercise and rest. The same is true spiritually: our strengths must be trained by intentional cycles of exercise (usage) and rest (restraint). Combine these two types of strength training

by taking a walk through a nature center, trail, or quiet road. Place your feet purposely, and make each step a prayerful journey.

2. As you walk, note the plants that you see. Ask God to give you insight into the "why" of the seasonal restraint He coded into plant DNA.

3. Think of a strength that is so natural you rarely filter its use. Exercise the discipline of restraint by resting that strength for a portion of your day or week. For example,

   • If you are quick to teach, be silent in a moment when others need to learn.

   • If you tend to volunteer for every cause, do not raise your hand this week, and allow others to fill (or not fill) the gaps.

   • If you are the team visionary, make room for someone else's dreams to grace the space.

   • If you are a skilled money manager, choose not to sway the budget discussion over a miscellaneous spending budget matter.

4. Journal how it felt to not do or not say what you were capable of doing or saying. Then refresh your memory with Jesus' example of restraint: "My time is not yet here" (John 7:6). Through prayer, submit your strengths to God's timing and will.

MENTAL WAITING

The past two chapters have forged a definition of the discipline of restraint based on the example of Jesus. Now we will explore three of the many applications of this discipline: mental waiting, earthly simplicity, and purity of soul.

A few years ago, severe flooding changed the shape of land and commerce near our prayer retreat home in Missouri. When the water receded from the main roads, Barry and I took a drive and were stunned by the sheer volume being released from the dam.

The rainbow over that deluge was beautiful. However, walking along the top of the dam, we were unable to hear anything, including each other, above the roaring waters.

Standing there, I realized that visually, dams at flood stage resemble waterfalls. But under the surface, there is always one critical difference between the two: control.

Our thoughts are much like roaring waters: a constantly in motion, "flowing something."[1] Mental waiting is like building a dam and exercising authority over the flow.

Why? Why control our mental flow? Why restrain such a creative force?

> Because undisciplined ability inevitably becomes abusive.
> Because the roar of many thoughts drowns out other voices.

Because the same God who volunteers to guide our steps is equally available to guide our thoughts.

Because, as mentioned previously, true intellectual strength is not just the ability to think, it is the ability to choose what to think and when to think. .

Jesus promised His followers that "when he, the Spirit of truth, comes, he will guide you into all the truth" (John 16:13).

We need a guide.
(It is a jungle up there.)

Practically, living led by the Spirit in our heads—mental waiting—can look something like this:

> *Why? I still don't know why he said that. We talked clearly about expectations. I said, "I can finish the project by the beginning of next month." But then he still acted disappointed and made that cutting comment in front of the guys. I can't believe that he—*
>
> *Wait. How many times have I replayed this in my head, just like that basket I missed back in college?*
>
> *Jesus, I'm self-leading again, aren't I? Holy Spirit, guide me into all the truth. Help me think with You. Are You initiating this rehash or am I? Well then: if I'm not supposed to go there in my head, where can I go? Yes, I can turn my thoughts to yesterday's message on generosity and pray for that family in the news that just lost their son.*

Taming and training our restless thought flow is strenuous. And mental peace is priceless.

> Great peace have those who love your law,
> and nothing can make them stumble. (Psalm 119:165)

You will keep in perfect peace
those whose minds are steadfast,
because they trust in you. (Isaiah 26:3)

The mind governed by the flesh is death, but the mind governed
by the Spirit is life and peace. (Romans 8:6)

GUIDED RESPONSE

Thought Focus:

Apply John 16:13 by asking the Holy Spirit to "lead you into all
the truth." In your head, defer to His leadership as you would to a
seasoned hiking guide through dangerous terrain. Ask, *Holy Spirit,
are You leading these thoughts?* And if He is not, turn your head-talk
in His direction.

Exercise:

1. In the last set of exercises, Psalm 139:13–16 reminded us that
   our every pore is saturated with God's fingerprints. How rich
   that the psalmist follows this celebration of God as Creator
   with a sincere request for God to search his heart.

   > Search me, God, and know my heart;
   >   test me and know my anxious thoughts.
   > See if there is any offensive way in me,
   >   and lead me in the way everlasting. (Psalm 139:23–24)

2. Keep this prayer near as you experiment with one or both
   of the following fasts that focus on the discipline of mental
   waiting.
   - Fast rehash of the past: When your thoughts are picking
     at an old wound or bullying you with past mistakes,
     discipline your mind to move in a totally different

direction. Yes, I am actually suggesting that in the
moment you do not pray directly for that situation or
quote scripture over that particular need. Instead, ask
the Holy Spirit to lead you to something "other" and
invest your mental strength, for example, in praying an
intercession for the lost, reading a book, singing a song,
or surprising someone with a special gift.

- Fast self-driven repentance: Instead of hunting down
  each misstep, quiet yourself in God's presence and
  ask the Holy Spirit to search your heart. If He brings
  something to your attention, thank Him and ask
  forgiveness. After a few minutes, if nothing comes to
  mind, thank Him and go on with your prayer time as
  opposed to circling around your soul like a hawk looking
  for hidden prey.

EARTHLY SIMPLICITY

As we turned the corner, Jonathan froze and Keona's eyes welled with tears. Even though weeks had passed since one of the largest tornados in history ravaged the city of Joplin, Missouri, the visible damage still left us speechless.

When Jonathan was asked to make a video for a group that was volunteering in Joplin, I printed out before and after pictures and a history of the city for us to discuss during the short road trip west. However, nothing apart from prior experience could have prepared us for what we saw on the ground.

The roads were clear, thanks to the efforts of volunteers and work crews, but I instinctively drove through the empty side streets as if we were part of a funeral procession. Slowly, our path led us to the site of a church. Solidly constructed with thick brick walls, the only intact piece of the entire building was the cross.

On the other side of the street, empty wheelchairs squeaked as the wind pushed them an inch here, an inch there in the empty space that once housed the elderly. The loss of life was beyond comprehension. Jonathan and Keona stood silently in the rubble, staring at the cross, while the symbol preached a powerful message:

> Few things endure.
> People are precious.
> Salvation is eternal.

Such are the foundational truths of earthly simplicity.

As a discipline of restraint, earthly simplicity recognizes our temporary residency on earth.

> Look around you.
> Do you see anything that is worth dying for?

As I type, I see the bedroom furniture my parents gifted to us, the hope chest Barry made for me, photos that capture treasured moments, and my comfy weathered boots by the nightstand. But the only things worth dying for are out of my sight but not out of my hearing. Jonathan is drumming on something, Louie is giggling with his guinea pigs, Keona's feet are dancing, and Barry is keeping the peace to "give Mommy a few more minutes to write."

> Lives are worth dying for.
> So, perhaps, life should receive more of our investment.

The rest is stuff—some of which is made more precious by memories or inheritance—but it is stuff nonetheless.

> What if we thinned the stuff and thickened the life?
> What if we uncluttered the man-made and freed up
> space for God-made?
> What might that space free within us?

⏸ GUIDED RESPONSE

Thought Focus:

Identify your most treasured possessions on earth by answering the question, "What things in my life are worth dying for?"

Exercise:

1. With a friend, read the following verse and select one or all of the proposed exercises to do together in the next few days.

   Do not store up for yourselves treasures on earth, where moths and vermin destroy, and where thieves break in and steal. But store up for yourselves treasures in heaven, where moths and vermin do not destroy, and where thieves do not break in and steal. For where your treasure is, there your heart will be also. (Matthew 6:19–21)

2. *Fast enough* +. In small, unannounced ways choose to only take what you need. Resist the urge to grab a chunk of napkins or a fistful of ketchup packets when you only need one. Put just enough on your plate instead of a reserve in case you want seconds. Defy the lure of two-for-one marketing or discounted additional purchases, and only purchase what you will actually use.

3. *Simplify your possessions.* Select a closet, cabinet, room, or bookcase (gasp) to thin. Ask yourself, "Is there something here that I do not truly need that could truly meet a need for someone else?" Donate quality "extra" to a community center, church, or family.

4. *Fast luxuries.* For a week, fast the purchase of luxuries. Keep a tally of how much you save by choosing water over designer coffee, staying home instead of eating out, or choosing not to buy another tune or app. At the end of the period, make a donation for that amount to a local cause that you have never given to previously.

[36]

PURITY OF SOUL

Consider the discipline of restraint inherent in Paul's counsel to the Corinthians:

> "I have the right to do anything," you say—but not everything is beneficial. "I have the right to do anything"—but I will not be mastered by anything. (1 Corinthians 6:12)

And again a few chapters later:

> "I have the right to do anything," you say—but not everything is beneficial. "I have the right to do anything"—but not everything is constructive. (1 Corinthians 10:23)

Liberty and lawlessness: Who knew that the latter could successfully masquerade as the former?

The Corinthians' early struggle is our daily struggle. In every age, followers of Jesus are in danger of rationalizing the pollution of their souls in the name of "freedom."

In both verses, *beneficial* is translated from συμφέρω (*sumphero*), which most often appears in my study Bible as "better" or "good." Paul could have made neutrality, as opposed to goodness, the standard, but the word *neutral* (as well as the concept it represents) is curiously absent in the Bible.

As the Corinthians were deciding what touched their bodies and infiltrated their minds, Paul counseled them to choose options that left a morally positive deposit in their souls.

Mastered comes from the Greek ἐξουσιάζω (*exousiazo*) and carries the meaning of gaining power over something or someone. Compartmentalization is a believer's enemy in this regard. In truth, everything we do affects all that we are. If the fruit of our "freedom" is the crescendo of controlling cravings and unholy appetites, we are self-deceived.

Constructive, from οἰκοδομέω (*oikodomeo*), is most often translated as some variation of the word *build*, such as in the phrase "build up." Christ-honoring freedom builds us up from the inside out by contributing to our spiritual health and growth.

In order for our choices to guard the purity of our souls, they must be morally positive, truth empowering, and internally edifying. In his letter, Paul explained that since Christ has purchased a believer's freedom, the exercising of that freedom must, therefore, honor Christ.

In other words, freedom is not king.

Personal freedom must bow to and be restrained by three timeless principles that cultivate purity of soul. The exercising of freedom must

1. be of genuine benefit to ourselves and others,
2. strengthen, not weaken, our will to obey God, and
3. build us up from within.

Purity of soul wages war against the anesthetizing spirit of deception that invites us to *use* our bodies instead of *steward* our bodies.

In our first reading for the discipline of restraint, we examined the equation *can* ≠ *should*. In our closing reading on this counterintuitive discipline, we see additionally that *can* ≠ *good*.

Whether in our minds (mental waiting), with our worldly possessions (earthly simplicity), or in our bodies (purity of soul), the discipline of restraint forges a faith that bends willingly to the timing of God and stands firmly for the honor of God.

⏸ GUIDED RESPONSE

Thought Focus:

Paul abhorred legalism. What is the difference between legalism and Paul's admonishment to refrain from permissible yet unbeneficial things?

Exercise:

1. Prayerfully personalize the following passage:

   > Do you not know that your bodies are temples of the Holy Spirit, who is in you, whom you have received from God? You are not your own; you were bought at a price. Therefore honor God with your bodies. (1 Corinthians 6:19–20)

2. Write down in detail how you spend your free time or me time. When you are not working, what fills your day? Include watching or playing sports, playing with children, hobbies, crafting, TV, gaming, social media, movies, texting, talking, going out with friends, magazines, books, working out, etc.

3. For the moment, expel the word *neutral* from your vocabulary, and, with God, evaluate each activity by the three principles Paul identified in 1 Corinthians. Then write your honest evaluations next to each activity. For example:
   - Savior, is this activity beneficial to others and to me?

- Does this practice in any way feed appetites that resist Your will and ways in my life?
- Does this choice spiritually build me up?

4. Estimate how much time you would free up daily by fasting something on your list that is clearly not beneficial (question 3a). Monitor how you respond to this suggestion. Stay present to any warfare that starts waging in your head. Risk pressing to the root and ask, "What in me resists the thought of a fast in this area?"

5. Then take a break from an activity that does not build you up spiritually (question 3c). For how long? Perhaps until you are no longer distracted by its absence. Fill that space with something that does build you up like a walk outside, a conversation with a God-loving friend, a new hobby, a great read, or music.

6. Throughout this process, consider the distinction between *escaping* and *relaxing* as you evaluate your recreational free time. If you realize that you are escaping, ask God for insight about what you are escaping from and why.

[Movement Nine]

A THEOLOGY OF TIME AND SPACE

> Spiritual life begins to decay when we fail to sense the grandeur of what is eternal in time. . . . Time and space are interrelated. To overlook either of them is to be partially blind. What we plead against is man's unconditional surrender to space, his enslavement to things. We must not forget that it is not a thing that lends significance to a moment; it is the moment that lends significance to things.[1]
>
> —ABRAHAM JOSHUA HESCHEL, *THE SABBATH*

WHAT YOU WILL NEED FOR THE EXERCISES

✔ Honest friends
✔ A notepad *or* journal
✔ Paper and markers *or* a computer
✔ Someone who has experienced burnout
✔ A blanket and a starry night

GIFT OR GRINCH?

Somehow, by some means, you woke up this morning. Maybe the scent of freshly ground coffee summoned a smile on your face, or warm sunlight gently invited you to experience a new day, or maybe not.

Maybe you jumped with a jolt from asleep to awake via a dog barking outside, a child's wail inside, a hidden phone ringing endlessly, an ambulance siren on the street, or—my least favorite of all options—an actual alarm clock that you, yourself, set on purpose.

By whatever method or madness, you are now awake, and I would like for you to reach back to the moment this morning when you first saw numbers on the clock and answer two questions:

1. How did you feel about time when you woke up this morning? As you glanced at the clock, did you think, *Ah, time, my faithful friend!* or, *Argh, time, my thieving foe!* Overall, do you tend to view time as a companion or a competitor? For you or against you? A gift or a grinch?

2. How did God feel about time when you woke up this morning? Was God standing there, bedside, with a stopwatch clenched in a tight fist, clicking it as soon as your eyes opened, and shouting, "On your mark, get set, go!" Or maybe tapping His foot, rolling His eyes, and saying through sarcastic, disappointed lips, "Oh, look, Gabriel. Look who decided to finally join the land of the living."

Or perhaps, just perhaps, God's eyes were resting on you, soaking up your features like a dad watching over his sleeping newborn with awe, and God's hand was slowly untying a bow on a carefully wrapped present called *today*.

Chapter 37 marks the beginning of the ninth movement in *The Sacred Slow*, toward a theology of time and space. Two truths about time can help us close the gap between our answer to question one and God's answer to question two.

Truth One: Time is pre-Fall.

In the beginning, God marked His creation by evenings and mornings: time celebrated the birth of life.

In the beginning, God set aside the seventh day as a Sabbath: time announced God's rhythm of rest.

In the beginning, God caused Adam to fall into a deep sleep while He formed Eve: time stood joyful watch while God prepared good gifts.

Time has always been a good part of God's creation. In fact, time is one of the only remaining original residents of Eden.

Truth Two: Time is a servant of sovereignty.

For years I have been intrigued with Solomon's perspective on time. A verse often quoted (even by souls who think that God had little to do with the writing of the Bible) is from Solomon's writings in Ecclesiastes 3:1:

> There is a time for everything,
>   and a season for every activity under the heavens.

> There's an opportune time to do things, a right time for everything on the earth. (THE MESSAGE)

To every thing there is a season, and a time to every purpose
under the heaven. (KJV)

The word that is translated *season* in the KJV and *time* in the
NIV and *The Message* only appears four times in the Old Testament.
In my study Bible, this word is twice translated "time," once "desig-
nated time," and once "time appointed."

Take a moment to weigh the word *time*. Solomon did not view
time as a countdown to doom. To this man endowed with divine wisdom, time was not a captive of chaos but rather a servant of sovereignty.

As we consider our beliefs regarding time over the next few chapters, may the God Who created time recalibrate our opinion of time.

> Teach us to number our days,
>> that we may gain a heart of wisdom.
>
> (from the prayer of Moses, Psalm 90:12)

⑪ GUIDED RESPONSE

Thought Focus:

Cultivate awareness of your feelings about time. Honestly formulate
a sentence that describes your working theology of time. Then ask
God if your perspective aligns with His own.

Exercise:

1. You get to take a poll! Make a list of people who interact
   with you in different contexts: at work, at church, in your
   home, in your neighborhood, or in your family (like brave
   parents, stubborn siblings, a fearless child, or a sassy spouse).
   Ask them for five minutes of their time to respond to a poll:

FROM YOUR PERSPECTIVE, CIRCLE ALL OPTIONS BELOW THAT YOU FEEL ARE SOMETIMES OR ALWAYS TRUE OF WHAT I SAY, WHAT I DO, OR HOW I ACT.		
Views time as something to beat	"There's just not enough hours in the day."	"We've got all the time in the world."
Is patient with processes	Regrets "lost" time	Is grateful for each day
Wishes the clock would stop	Views time as a gift	Is always rushing
"Take your time."	Rested	Regularly feels behind
Whether early or late, still arrives stressed	At peace with the clock	Has time to spare
Longs for simpler days	Lives at a healthy pace	Good with time management
"Hurry up! We don't have all day."	"Time keeps on slippin' slippin', slippin' into the future . . ."	Is disappointed in others when they "waste time"

2. Resist the urge to deflect ("Well, you're kind, but I'm not always that way."), dilute ("I used to say that, but now I don't."), or defend ("What?! That's your issue, not mine.") Just let the participants mark the poll in peace and then take their responses into prayer.

3. Journal what God may be revealing to you through this exercise.

THE FLOW OF TIME

"You know that the ocean has currents?" my neighbor Tad began. "Well, so does air. An airplane in the sky is sort of like a submarine in the water. Sometimes the current is fast or slow, smooth or choppy. That's what causes what you describe as 'lumpy air.'"

"Air flow is chartable," my friend Erik added. "For example, in winter, the jet stream migrates south, and you know it will take longer to fly west than the same route east. Air streams don't just go straight; there are dips and valleys. Anything that changes the direction of the wind causes turbulence. When the winter wind hits the mountains at a 90-degree angle, it creates turbulence. When the summer heat warms up the ground air, you can expect turbulence when you land in Phoenix."

I am grateful for patient pilot friends who have offered visual explanations for an otherwise invisible phenomenon. Though no pilot or seafarer would claim that the skies or the oceans can be tamed, captains in the air and on the waters confirm that patterns can still be observed, described, and taken into account when making plans.

The same can be said of time. While it is true that time cannot be tamed, it does have patterns that can be observed, rhythms that can be described, and flow that can be accounted for as we shape the space of our lives.

As a practice, charting the flow of time can transition us from living in a state of continual surprise when patterns repeat themselves, to living in anticipation of familiar rhythms; from living one step behind, perpetually catching up, to living attentive and flexible, at peace with life's pace.

For some, this type of aerial-view thinking will be easy; for others it will be extremely difficult. If you find yourself in the latter group, please call a friend for support: this principle is too critical to skip.

The guided response exercise that follows will help you chart a year, but as an example, I will chart one aspect of how time flows for me within a twenty-four-hour period.

Time is represented on the horizontal axis and strength on the vertical axis. This simple line graph depicts the flow of my mental strength throughout the day. As you can see, my clarion hours are in the morning. I take a (massive) dip in the afternoon and pep back up a bit in the evening. Yes, there are exceptions, but this pattern has been true of me for decades. Before I recognized the flow, I was frustrated by low productivity in the afternoons. Now I work with this pattern in shaping my space.

Daily Time-Flow

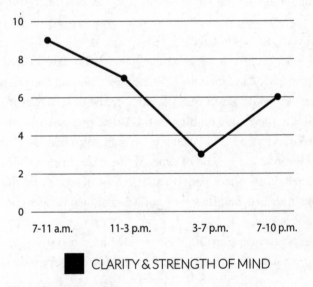

CLARITY & STRENGTH OF MIND

For example, by looking at the chart, when would you recommend that I plan to check in on homework with my teen? Write? Clean the house? Spend time with a friend? Run errands? Watch a movie with my youngest? Relax by playing cards with my husband? Do finances?

(Please let me know if you figure out that last one.)

Am I always able to position each task in its dream space? No. But identifying the flow helps me adjust my expectations, especially when the match of time and task is less than ideal.

My point is this: since time is a God-gift, its flow is to be studied, appreciated, and called on to steward our lives. Imagine the wisdom hidden in these patterns. Imagine what insights could be gained into my family if I layered the same flow chart for my husband and children over mine. The potential is substantial.

Books abound on time management. But if we seek to manage time without first studying the flow of time, our successes may be short lived.

My God, I pray for the souls holding this book.
Create space for them. Grant them an aerial view.
May they begin to discover patterns in their lives
spiritually, emotionally, and relationally.
May they discern rhythms that affect work, home, and
self-perceptions.
Mostly, may they grow in appreciation for this gift called
time and invest each moment in love for You, amen.

⏸ GUIDED RESPONSE

Thought Focus:
Become aware of what people and tasks are (1) the glad recipients of your clarion hours of the day and (2) the default recipients of

your lowest energy hours of the day. If the distribution does not reflect your values, make a step toward shaping your space by taking increased authority over the stewardship of time.

Exercise:

1. This is going to be fun. Make a chart with the next twelve months represented on the x-axis and a scale of 0–10 on the y-axis (see my example on the next page). Layering the time-flow of an entire group is an insightful tool to increase health and understanding in relationships. However, for this exercise, we will consider the many hats of just one soul—yours.

2. List the roles you fill. For example, I am a wife, mom, writer, speaker, mentor, and nonprofit executive director. For each role, chart the flow of task intensity (from a low of 0 to a high of 10) over the next twelve months.

3. Add to this chart any seasonal emotional dips or peaks that you (or close friends) may recognize.

4. Then step back and attempt an objective evaluation.
   - Are there spaces where too many high-task seasons overlap? How does that overlap affect you? How does that overlap affect those closest to you? Can you thin the overlap by releasing responsibilities or asking for help?
   - How might emotional dips and peaks be affecting your performance at work? Your peace at home?
   - In which seasons would it be wise to refuse additional assignments?

5. Search for space. Instead of filling it, plan how to protect it and let it breathe.

6. As in the reading, I will offer an example from my time-flow evaluations. Please note that this chart would have looked very different two decades ago, so you may need to revisit this exercise in the future as your seasons shift.

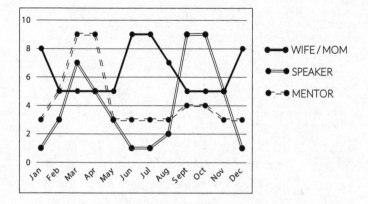

Understanding the time-flow of different responsibilities has empowered my family to shape space in a way that avoids too many tasks peaking simultaneously.

- Mothering, obviously, for me is constant, but my responsibilities increase when school is out or Barry is leading men's prayer retreats.
- Mentoring is another constant in my life, but each March–April is especially intense as I conclude one Mentoring Encounter and begin the next with a new group of leaders. The intensity of my role as an executive director mirrors the mentoring time-flow.
- Regarding speaking, we take the kids' vacation schedules into account and avoid extended speaking engagements in the summer or winter holidays.
- As we grow and hats come and go, this flow fluctuates. But an aerial view continues to benefit my family as we shape our space to live strong in spirit, soul, and body.

MARGIN

"I'm so tired of feeling tired."
"Everywhere I turn, someone needs me."
"That's it. I'm done. I have nothing left to give."
*"If something doesn't change soon, I'm afraid I'll burn out
or completely collapse."*

Do any of these statements sound familiar? When uttered sincerely, such phrases may be indicators of exhaustion. They certainly were for me early on in my marriage. Barry and I had been burning the candle at both ends for more than a decade. As single campus ministers (he was in Texas and I was in Western Australia), we stayed up late, ate irregularly, exercised infrequently, always said yes, and never thought about it because we were so very thrilled to partner with Jesus in His love for the world. When we married, we continued this pace as we poured out our lives for the love of university students.

Then a transition occurred, and we needed to spend one year in constant travel to gather a team of committed individuals and churches who would partner with us in the next season of ministry. Many may be familiar with this model of missionary itineration. The rationale behind the practice is that it keeps the faces and focuses of missionaries fresh in the minds of those who support them and it provides the opportunity for others to consider God's global cause.

In theory, it is truly beautiful. In practice, it is insane unless you happen to be graced with hyperactivity and outrageous extroversion.

I am not.

As the miles clicked on the odometer, something else was clicking within me—a countdown to burnout.

Within six months, I was a zombie. Living out of a suitcase, having intimate conversations with people who were absolute strangers less than an hour before, searching for hotels at midnight, and eating way too many breakfast specials did not make for healthy living for my wiring, physically or emotionally.

Genetically far sturdier, Barry was tired but not at the point of collapse. When he heard me crying in the kitchen, he came running to find his wife gripping the counter and unable to speak through her tears. He saw no signs of accident or injury. There was no opened letter with sad news. All he could do was hold me.

Finally, I was able to sputter out, "There are dir-dir-dirty di-di-dishes in the si-si-ink."

The dishes did me in.

This was clearly a case of no margin.

Margin is a concept I first encountered through the writings of Dr. Richard Swenson.[1] Though I rarely use print space to summarize principles when I know that others have already skillfully written about them, Dr. Swenson's concept of margin is one my husband and I ask every person we mentor to absorb.

Picture a straight line representing 100 percent of your daily supply of emotional, physical, interpersonal, and spiritual strength. On that line, place three points: A at the beginning, B at 75 percent and C at 100 percent.

Daily Energy

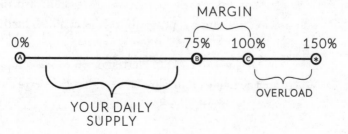

According to Dr. Richard Swenson, on a normal day God intends for us to live between points A and B. The space between points B and C (which he calls margin) is a reserve to be saved up for crises, the unexpected, and the extra mile.

However, we tend to expend A to C (100 percent of our energy) each day by using up the B–C reserve in normal living. So when a crisis does occur, we have nothing to draw from and are pushed into overload. When overload extends, burnout or breakdown begins.

On paper, it is clear: the madness must stop. In practice, however, making margin a discipline can be a complicated venture, especially in contexts that applaud the exhausted and commend the depleted for their "sacrificial giving."

⏸ GUIDED RESPONSE

Thought Focus:

Ask yourself if any of the four starting sentences of this chapter sound familiar to you or a loved one. If so, intervene. If change feels impossible or overwhelming, invest time and money in an appointment with a wise friend or life coach. Doing nothing will be far more costly.

Exercise:

1. Conduct an interview with someone who understands burnout firsthand. Ask if they are able to identify any factors that contributed to their exhaustion. Do they have any thoughts or suggestions from their journey regarding practices that would help safeguard a soul against this level of debilitating weariness?

2. Draw out Dr. Swenson's ABC illustration from the reading. Where are you living on this line? Do you have a reserve built up emotionally? Physically? Spiritually?

3. If so, what has helped build that reserve? If not, what is draining that reserve?

4. If you are currently in overload or burnout, ask for the practical support of friends and make an appointment with your doctor. Exhaustion can quickly descend into clinical depression, and many will affirm that the road back to health from exhaustion-induced depression is a painfully long trek.

SPACE-SHAPING SABOTEURS

If margin is a true need for health on all levels of our existence, and if time is a gift with discernible rhythm and chartable flow, clearly we need to exercise authority and shape the space of our lives in a way that honors the gift's Giver. Toward this end, wisdom invites us to be wary of four saboteurs of space-shaping (especially if we live in driven cultures that mistake margin for laziness).

Inflexible schedules. Think of a schedule as you would a fishing boat. Like other concepts we have considered in *The Sacred Slow*, a boat is a means, not an end. Boats are valuable in direct proportion to their ability to facilitate journey. A boat is good to the extent that it serves its owner's purposes.

Likewise, a schedule is a means that assists us in our journey through life. Good ones serve their owners as opposed to making servants out of their owners.

As fishing boats are crafted to ride the ups and downs of lakes and seas, so, too, schedules should be crafted to absorb the natural ebbs and flows of real life. Rigid schedules are self-defeating. One of my wise friends, Stephanie Smith, once compared inflexible schedules to heavy metal trains, bound to immovable tracks, determined to keep going—even when they find themselves underwater.

Superman Time Syndrome. Perhaps Superman can fly to the store and be back in fifteen minutes, but Clark Kent needs an hour.

Superman Time Syndrome (STS) is a somewhat humorous saboteur that entertained my husband and me early on in our marriage.

Barry, a servant-hearted optimist, would say, "We need milk. I'll be back in fifteen minutes." I, an accuracy-obsessed realist, would reply, "Babe, how is that humanly possible, given that H.E.B. [it is a Texas thing] is eight miles away?" Silence. Chuckles. Then with a wink, Bear would counter, "You're right. I'll be back in ten minutes."

Another manifestation of STS is estimating with utopian factors: "Well, I could have mailed that package in twenty minutes if the lights had all been green, and there hadn't been a crazy line, and the insanely slow person in front of me had just stayed home, and the post office computer system wasn't as old as Moses . . ."

It is one thing to make a rough estimate, but it is quite another thing to be in the habit of (shall we just say it?) lying about how much time tasks require.

How long do you guess a certain responsibility might take? Multiply that number by two if you are a realist and by three if you are an optimist and shape your space accordingly.

Refusing to pay the price of disappointment. Someone somewhere is going to be disappointed about something no matter what we do. People who go beyond mere disappointment and are actually disappointed *in us* because we said no to their requests would probably have found a reason to be disappointed in us even if we had said yes. How often do we say yes to such sour souls in a vain effort to please them, prove that we are team players, or "honor" them into accepting us?

A dear family friend, Carol Arnold, once told me, "Alicia, people come with their stuff. They are going to leave with their stuff. You didn't give it to them. You can't take it away."

Indeed.

We take a step toward emotional health and the strength to

shape our space when we choose not to take personal responsibility for someone else's interior discontentment.

The nth degree. When your report would have been complete hours ago apart from your search for just the right font; when guests are about to visit, and you find yourself using an old toothbrush to clean a part of your bathroom that *no one* has seen since the home was constructed; when you are asked to bring something to the office party and instead of running by the store, you spend six hours creating something "unique"; when you agonize over e-mails, evaluating them from every angle before pressing send . . . you could be in bondage to the nth degree.

Let it go.

It does not have to be perfect.

Neither the font nor the toilet can say, "I love you." (Invest your time in someone who can.)

⏸ GUIDED RESPONSE

Thought Focus:
Next time you want to decline a request but feel pressure to say yes, take the tension into God's presence and ask for wisdom. Journal any insights you receive.

Exercise:
As we conclude our ninth movement, select at least two of the following exercises to help you grow in stewardship of God's gift of time.

1. Lay a blanket outside on a starry night. Stare up at the sky and consider how God shaped space.
2. Stare at your daily calendar. Honestly assess if you are a slave to your schedule or if your schedule is a servant of your values.

3. Listen for Superman Time Syndrome in the voices of those near you. Instead of pointing out the space-shaping saboteur in their lives, reflect on what could be motivating this illogical yet protected delusion regarding time.
4. Be satisfied with good. Next time your natural wiring seeks to unnecessarily go above and beyond, resist the nth degree and choose to steward your strength.

UNEXPECTED FRIENDS

> In winter are we bare? Yes.
>
> In winter are we barren? No.
>
> True life still is.
>
> The Father's work in us does not sleep—though in spiritual winters he retracts all advertisement. And when he does so, he is purifying our faith, strengthening our character, conserving our energy, and preparing us for the future.
>
> The sleepy days of winter hide us so that the seductive days of summer will not ruin us.[1]
>
> —ALICIA BRITT CHOLE, *ANONYMOUS: JESUS' HIDDEN YEARS . . . AND YOURS*

WHAT YOU WILL NEED FOR THE EXERCISES

✔ Three to five individuals whose lives inspire you to walk more closely with Jesus
✔ A notepad *or* journal
✔ A Bible
✔ Walking shoes
✔ Someone who exemplifies the gift of wisdom

WHERE FOLLOW LEADS

"Self is such a terrible thing," my mentor began in a soft voice still graced with the rich sounds of her beloved Germany. I met Sister Rebekka in 1994 during my first extended prayer retreat. Every year since, she has gifted me with her time and her prayers. Her words are weighty and her life even weightier. I readied my pen as ninety years of wisdom took an anticipatory breath.

"What now occupies much of my thinking," she continued, "is this amazing word: *follow* Me. Yes, this has begun to stare at me."

My pen paused, stilled by the realization that even separated by an ocean and four decades we were focused on the same words in the Scriptures.

"'*Follow Me*,' Jesus says," her voice slowed. "'*Follow Me* into weakness. *Follow Me* into suffering.' You think it would be to a nice place. But there is something of the cross for me." The phone fell silent for a few heavy seconds. Then my dear Sister Rebekka concluded, "'*Follow Me*,' He says. So, yes, I go."

"'Come, follow me,' Jesus said, 'and I will send you out to fish for people'" (Matthew 4:19). Where did we think Jesus' invitation would lead us?

The One we follow was familiar with obscurity and waiting, betrayal and slander, injustice and rejection, and physical and emotional suffering. Yet somehow we think that following Jesus means that we will avoid such pain.

But *follow* is not about scenery. *Follow* is all about company.

The very things we would opt to avoid may be the unexpected friends that keep our focus on *follow*.

The very things that prompt us to question God's existence may be the unexpected friends that keep us in His presence.

"Self is such a terrible thing."

And death to self rarely comes covered in confetti.

⏸ GUIDED RESPONSE

Thought Focus:

Where did you think Jesus' "Follow Me" would lead you? Bring any unexpected places in your journey into prayer and ask, *God, whether or not my mind can comprehend Your response, I ask You to comfort me with the certainty of Your presence in this part of my journey.*

Exercise:

1. Think of three to five people whose trustworthy lives inspire you to walk more closely with Jesus. Call them with some version of this question: "Your life makes me hungry to know God more. If you have some time, could you briefly share what experiences God has used to form you into the person you are today?"

2. After all the interviews, compare notes. Are there any uniquenesses? Any commonalities?

3. If someone were to honor you with a call like this today, what answers would you give?

AN ANCIENT ANGST

Why did God allow this?

Whether wondered in prayer, thought with trembling, or yelled at the heavens, this weighty question often sounds in the place of pain.

We ask this about the faithful father killed in a car accident, but less often about the drunk driver who also died.

We ask this about the young woman who lost her sight, but less often about the addict who lost her home.

We ask this about the child born with brain damage, but less often about the smoker who contracted lung cancer.

Because at its core, "Why did God allow this?" is a questioning of God's justice. When choice triggers consequence and sin triggers suffering, we sadly acknowledge the realities of sowing and reaping. But when suffering just comes, we struggle to make sense of the story.

Fully comprehending our infinite God's answer to our *why* is obviously beyond us. But God has revealed pieces and parts of His answer through His Son's experience on earth.

During the days of Jesus' life on earth, he offered up prayers and petitions with fervent cries and tears to the one who could save him from death, and he was heard because of his reverent submission. Son though he was, he learned obedience from what he suffered and, once made perfect, he became the source of eternal salvation for all who obey him. (Hebrews 5:7–9)

When we think of Jesus' suffering, we rightly pin it to our sins. The writer of Hebrews, however, revealed other outcomes of suffering in Jesus' life.

The innocent One *cultivated reverent submission* through His sufferings. (v. 7)

The submitted One *learned obedience* through His sufferings. (v. 8)

The obedient One *was made perfect*—matured and completed— through His sufferings. (v. 9)

On this side of eternity, there may be no means of simplifying, let alone resolving, the age-old angst toward suffering. However, mystery invites us to find comfort in the knowledge that suffering holds for us the same power it did for Jesus to cultivate submission, grow obedience, and bring maturity to faith.

What turns pain into power is *perspective*.

⏸ GUIDED RESPONSE

Thought Focus:

In the last chapter, we asked God to infuse our spirits with a certainty of His presence in the more unexpected parts of our journey. In this chapter, we will ask God to reveal what He desires to grow in us through such times. In prayer, ask God for His perspective on your pain.

Exercise:

Though the why may elude us, the fruit does not: Suffering holds hidden treasures for all who follow Jesus. Suffering is an unexpected friend. Prayerfully consider the following quotes and then journal your response to the last prompt.

1. A prison prayer from Jeanne Guyon:

   The stones of my prison looked in my eyes like rubies; I esteemed them more than all the gaudy brilliance of a vain world. My heart was full of that joy which You give to those who love You in the midst of their greatest crosses.[1]

2. On the mystery of suffering from the apostle Paul:

   Now I rejoice in what I am suffering for you, and I fill up in my flesh what is still lacking in regard to Christ's afflictions, for the sake of his body, which is the church. (Colossians 1:24)

3. The advice of a senior demon to a junior demon regarding how to snare the soul of a young Christian from the fiction of C. S. Lewis:

   Do not be deceived, Wormwood. Our cause is never more in danger than when a human, no longer desiring, but still intending, to do our Enemy's will, looks round upon a universe from which every trace of Him seems to have vanished, asks why he has been forsaken, and still obeys.[2]

4. I believe that suffering is _____

   _____

   _____

THE SILENCE OF GOD

My heart racing, I ran down the hall toward the gut-wrenching cry in the far bedroom. About to open the door, I froze, realizing that my eldest was in prayer.

"God, help me!!" Jonathan cried on the other side of the closed door. His voice, though desperate, lacked anger. This was not the cry of a soul taunting God. This was the cry of a soul seeking God.

The ground felt holy as I held my breath and heard Jonathan ask for two things. His first pain-inspired request was, "God, please give me one day without Asperger's. Just one day to know what my life would be like without special needs."

Jonathan is a magnificent soul, a wondrous blend of earnestness, brilliance, creativity, and justice. From the beginning, we have taught our son that Asperger's enables him to see the world in a unique way and make a much-needed contribution to his generation, and that all strengths have shadows.

Jonathan gratefully acknowledges the gifts, but sometimes the shadows are so deep that he would trade all the strengths in a heartbeat to simply feel "normal." Listening, I was thankful once again that the strengths of Asperger's are so tangible and quantifiable, so unlike what Jonathan asked for next.

"God, please," he continued through tears, "please speak to me. I wish I could hear You speak to me. Why can't I hear Your voice?"

Jonathan had heard our voices. He wanted to hear God's voice. But, like me, Jonathan has never heard the audible voice of God.

We both are still listening.

I stared at the closed door and waited for a miracle. God can speak. God can heal. God can do anything He desires. Perhaps in response to childlike faith?

The closed door muffled the only sounds Jonathan and I would hear that afternoon: his sobs. Giving Jonathan and Jesus their privacy, I walked softly back to the reading chair and stared out the window. "Jesus, if You were ever going to speak audibly to Jonathan," I offered, "now would be a good time."

Sitting in the same silence as my son a few rooms away, I wondered how I was going to explain God's silence to one so young. Preparing myself for the inevitable discussion to come, I brought to mind what I knew to be true about the unexpected friend of God's silence:

> Countless believers have affirmed through the ages
> that God's silence purifies our love for Him.
> God is good. All that He does is for our good.
> Therefore, we can be confident that even when it is the last
> thing we want to hear, God's silence works God's good in us.

The closed door creaked open as I heard a soft, "Mom, can we talk?"

"Yes, my love," I responded, rising from the chair and gathering my tools: a Bible, a box of tissues, and a shared ache that will be gloriously satisfied when Jesus' voice summons us to the other side.

⓿ GUIDED RESPONSE

Thought Focus:

Though my son was wrestling with the absence of God's audible voice, "the silence of God" is often used to describe seasons of spiritual drought when all we seem to be able to hear is silence. John of the Cross is often quoted as saying, "Silence is God's first language."[1] Consider this thought in relation to the creation account. When did God speak? When was God silent?

Exercise:

1. Ask someone who exemplifies the gift of wisdom why they sometimes choose to be silent when others would prefer them to speak.

2. Add your own responses. Think of your interactions with a child or close friend. When do you choose silence over speech?

3. From the combined responses, cross off anything that would be inconsistent with God's character (e.g., "because they are driving me nuts"), and prayerfully think about what remains.

4. Pick up your Bible and contrast the Voice that sounded from heaven at Jesus' baptism (Matthew 3:17) and the silence of Father God that accompanied Jesus during His temptation (Matthew 4:1–11). If possible, go outside for a walk and reflect on what purposes God's speech and silence might have served in each context.

A FRIEND CALLED FAILURE

For years, the words circled about in my head, struggling to find a solid place to land in my working theology. I could say other phrases with ease like, "Pain is not purposeless" and, "Weakness opens up new depths of worship."

But this phrase? Something about its utterance—let alone its acceptance—hurt.

Today, even though my head and heart are in agreement, the words still spill out slowly: *I am sincerely grateful for my failures.*

"Failures? You mean missteps or growth curves, right?"

No. I mean failures.

"Well, then certainly you mean ethically neutral failures as opposed to sin-induced failures, right?"

No. I mean both. But I will start with the easier one.

I am grateful for my ethically neutral, professional failures: for the declined article submissions, the books that never "hit," and the works that went out of print because poor sales did not warrant a publisher's continued investment.

Grateful? Yes.

Giddy? No.

It hurts. Each "your book is being discontinued" letter hurt.

A lot.

With one word, God could have chosen to grant increase in any of the situations. But my good and perfect Father chose to allow doors to close (or slam) as my fingers got out of the way (most of the time).

Professional failures have been gifts to me. The unanswerable questions keep me focused on obedience—instead of fruit—as the true tell of both my love for God and my spiritual health. The inherent disappointment keeps me tender to God's Spirit and small in my own eyes, both of which safeguard my soul.

Now for the harder one.

I am grateful for my sin-inspired failures: for the closed doors my self-protection triggered and the embarrassment my pain-filled self-defensiveness invited.

> Am I grateful that I sinned? No.
> But I am grateful for the failures that resulted from
> my sin.

Why? Because denial has no healing power.

Many years ago, I went to the after-hours clinic with an unusually high fever. The discerning doctor on duty ordered a strange assortment of tests that revealed a collection of questionable masses, which led to a quickly scheduled surgery. The fever was simply a manifestation of—not the creator of—interior malfunction. Without the fever, I might have gone many more months without discovering what was within me.

Sin-induced failure is like a fever. Its purpose is to alert us to the presence of something that needs spiritual attention. This second type of failure is a manifestation of—not a creator of—sin. Such failures reveal internal dysfunction and force us to pause and take responsibility for what is within us. Whether in our bodies or our souls, ignoring failure can be lethal.

In its many forms, failure can become an unexpected friend. In fact, failure is often one of the wisest teachers in the growth process—if we ever let it speak.

⏸ GUIDED RESPONSE

Thought Focus:

One of my sons showed signs of perfectionism very early in life. Consequently, he has heard this phrase from me countless times: Mistakes are our friends. Mistakes help us learn.

Exercise gratitude as you think about lessons learned from mistakes and failures.

Exercise:

1. This is an exercise in sobriety, not spin. To learn from failure is to value humility, truth, conviction, and growth. People have different responses to failure, ranging from promptly forgetting it (denial) to wallowing in it (self-punishment). How would you describe your first response to both ethically neutral and sin-induced failure on the continuum below?

DENIAL   SELF PUNISHMENT

O————————————————O

I deny that I have failed   I beat myself up
in order to avoid the pain   with my failures

2. What has failure taught you about yourself? About God?
3. Reflect on Jesus' words to Peter spoken hours before Peter's infamous denial:

"Simon, Simon, Satan has asked to sift all of you as wheat. But I have prayed for you, Simon, that your faith may not fail. And when you have turned back, strengthen your brothers."

But he replied, "Lord, I am ready to go with you to prison and to death." (Luke 22:31–33)

4. Imagine yourself in Peter's place and hear Jesus' words from two different moments in time: (1) as the sincere, confident Peter prior to Jesus' arrest, and (2) as the sincere, broken Peter after denying Jesus thrice. Think of how Peter might have interpreted these words differently pre-failure and post-failure.

SABBATH AND PRAYER RETREATS

> " Sadly, everything about us works against slowing down. Our compulsion to produce and not waste time invades the space God gave for us to rest. . . . Sabbath is God's way of saying, "Stop. Notice your limits. Don't burn out."[1]
>
> —ADELE AHLBERG CALHOUN,
> *SPIRITUAL DISCIPLINES HANDBOOK*

WHAT YOU WILL NEED FOR THE EXERCISES

✔ Internet access *or* a magazine
✔ A Bible
✔ A notepad *or* journal
✔ A sheet of paper and a dark marker or crayon
✔ Friends
✔ Your calendar
✔ An inspiring book
✔ A small bag

THE WORK OF REST

One happy Monday, I had the joy of spending a few hours with my dear Aunt Sylvia in San Jose, California. After a wonderful meal of Indian food, we stopped by her house, and the first thing I noticed was a row of stunning, strong sunflowers lining her driveway. She said, "Oh, those? They're volunteers. They'll last the whole summer."

> I have planted sunflowers.
> Most withered pitifully.
> A few grew decently.
> None flowered all summer.
> And I have *never* had volunteers.

Sabbath rest is more like my sunflowers than those of my dear Aunt Sylvia. Sabbath rarely volunteers itself. It does not simply appear and grow strong on its own accord. Sabbath requires careful planning, repeated planting, and constant protection.

In other words: it takes *work* to experience sabbath *rest*. It takes *planning* to let space *breathe*.

Throughout the ages, many have carefully prepared to obey the fourth commandment: houses are scrubbed, food is prepared, clothes are laundered, and candles are in place before the sun sets each Friday evening.

Though today's diverse manifestations of applied sabbath are many, Exodus 20:8–10 still demands a sincere response: "Remember the Sabbath day by keeping it holy. Six days you shall labor and do all your work, but the seventh day is a sabbath to the LORD your God."

Honoring a day of sabbath rest requires both discipline to prepare in advance and trust that six days of work will provide for seven days of living. Though costly, such disciplined trust works for our good. As Jesus explained, "The Sabbath was made for man, not man for the Sabbath" (Mark 2:27).

Evidently, God modeled and created sabbath space because mankind needed sabbath space.

Resting is a form of obedience, and obedience opens the way to greater nearness with God.

As you reflect on your practice of sabbath-keeping, consider the following sabbath prayer by Claiborne, Wilson-Hartgrove, and Okoro:

> *Lord of Creation,*
> *create in us a new rhythm of life*
> *composed of hours that sustain rather than stress,*
> *of days that deliver rather than destroy,*
> *of time that trickles rather than tackles.*
>
> *Lord of Liberation,*
> *by the rhythm of your truth, set us free*
> *from the bondage and baggage that break us,*
> *from the Pharaohs and fellows who fail us,*
> *from the plans and pursuits that prey upon us.*
>
> *Lord of Resurrection,*
> *may we be raised into the rhythm of your new life,*
> *dead to deceitful calendars,*
> *dead to fleeting friend requests,*
> *dead to the empty peace of our accomplishments.*

To our packed-full planners, we bid, "Peace!"
To our over-caffeinated consciences, we say, "Cease!"
To our suffocating selves, Lord, grant release.

Drowning in a sea of deadlines and death chimes,
we rest in you our lifeline.
By your ever-restful grace,
allow us to enter your Sabbath rest
as your Sabbath rest enters into us.

In the name of our Creator, our Liberator, our Resurrection
and life we pray. Amen[1]

GUIDED RESPONSE

Thought Focus:

Remember the Sabbath day by keeping it holy. Six days you shall labor and do all your work, but the seventh day is a sabbath to the LORD your God. On it you shall not do any work, neither you, nor your son or daughter, nor your male or female servant, nor your animals, nor any foreigner residing in your towns. For in six days the LORD made the heavens and the earth, the sea, and all that is in them, but he rested on the seventh day. Therefore the LORD blessed the Sabbath day and made it holy. (Exodus 20:8–11)

With God, honestly process any personal struggles or successes in honoring this fourth commandment.

Exercise:

Graphic designers view space as an artistic element. Space is intentional. Space helps non-space breathe and speak.

Likewise, God as our Designer crafted us to need space in our lives. In the beginning He designed the gift of time to contain night (space to sleep) and set apart the seventh day as Sabbath (space to rest).

Without space, our minds become restless and our relationships become brittle. Without space, we reduce our bodies to assets instead of respecting our bodies as temples.

1. Visit a website or pull out a magazine that you find appealing. Consider the purposes of "white space" and margins on the website or printed page.
2. Next, leave anything electronic behind and bring your Bible, a journal, a dark crayon, and a clean piece of paper to a quiet place.
3. Ponder the following verse slowly: "By the seventh day God had finished the work he had been doing; so on the seventh day he rested from all his work. Then God blessed the seventh day and made it holy" (Genesis 2:2–3).
4. Reflecting on steps 1 and 3 above, place a blank sheet of paper before you and color the paper, leaving a margin to reflect how much sabbath "white space" you actually have in your week. Remember that escaping is not synonymous with resting. Escaping numbs. Resting renews.
5. Place the paper before you and prayerfully listen for any impressions regarding ways God desires you to grow or expand in sabbath rest.

COME AWAY

The surrounding sentences faded as I became captivated by a simple string of words. Though less than a sentence, this phrase has proven to be more than enough adventure for a lifetime. The writer, Henri Nouwen, encouraged his readers to take a retreat devoted to prayer, "an hour a day, an afternoon a week, a day a month, a week a year."[1] I closed my eyes, savoring this phrase alongside Jesus' invitation recorded in Mark 6:31: "Come with me by yourselves to a quiet place and get some rest."

An hour a day devoted to resting with Jesus was familiar, thanks to the teaching and example of early mentors. An afternoon a week was familiar, thanks to unanswerable questions that inspired a practice of prayerfully waiting on God one afternoon a week in a lonely university chapel.

But one full day every month and one full week every year? What a magnificent thought.

Decades later, how can I begin to quantify how much implementing these disciplines has meant to me? Their weight is beyond measure.

The monthly prayer retreats became a true discipline when Barry and I married. On our wedding bands we engraved the following: *for His Name and His honor, for His glory and His kingdom.* We knew that intentionality would be needed to honor that commitment, so over the years we developed the habit of giving each other twenty-four-hour spaces to rest alone with Jesus.

The discipline of extended prayer retreats began for me in my seventh year of ministry. The first took place over nine days in an Arizona desert. Even though now, as a mom of three, the time frame is much shorter, that place—that rich desert space—has become a spiritual home to which I return annually.

Not for sermon prep or writing or admin or catch-up, I view these set-apart spaces like the expensive perfume poured out on Jesus' feet before His betrayal (Matthew 26:6–7). These retreats are love offerings: gifts with no strings attached. Neither to receive an answer nor to resolve a problem, the retreats are for whispering, "I love You."

As I have already mentioned, it takes work to create space to rest. There are schedules to rearrange, responsibilities to move about, budgets to consider, and to-dos to postpone, delegate, or leave undone. But without question, the work is worth it.

Barry and the kids all agree that I return from prayer retreats with greater clarity, patience, and joy. Barry returns with a renewed perspective and the contentment that can only come from hearing Father God's affirmation, "This is My son, whom I love."

Your season and schedule may lead you to develop quarterly retreats and monthly Saturday afternoon spaces for prayer, or annual weekends and weekly Monday mornings, etc. Whatever their configuration, what makes these spaces rich is *intentionality* and *regularity*.

Plan for them.
Schedule them.
Guard them as you would any meeting with a king.

⏸ GUIDED RESPONSE

Thought Focus:
"But what would I do?"

"I'm afraid I wouldn't hear anything."

"To be honest, it's too painful to get still, which is why
I keep moving."

Beyond the details of schedules and finances, what common
objections might prevent you from embarking on a prayer-retreat
adventure?

Exercise:

1. My dream is that prayer retreating becomes a regular discipline
   in your life, a monthly pause that grows into a treasured given
   in your schedule.[2] To begin, invest in dream-inspiring research.
   Connect with your friends and ask:
   - Has anyone taken a personal prayer retreat?
   - If so, how did you set aside time? How did you spend
     the time?
   - Any suggestions for places to go for a retreat?
   - What one book (other than the Bible) would you bring
     on a prayer retreat?
2. Get practical with Jesus. What would it take for the two of
   you to experience a twenty-four-hour retreat?
   - Look at your calendar together. Circle several dates that
     are possibilities over the next few months.
   - List details that would need to be covered: Walking the
     dog? Finding someone to fill in at church? Postponing a
     meeting or a deadline?
   - Especially if finances are a factor, consider what it would
     take to stay and pray at home without distractions.
3. Ask God to help you take the next step. Your Father longs to
   give you good and perfect gifts.

PACKING LIGHT

> Immediately Jesus made his disciples get into the boat and go on ahead of him to Bethsaida, while he dismissed the crowd. After leaving them, he went up on a mountainside to pray. (Mark 6:45–46)

Even if taking a prayer retreat seems like a distant dream, this discipline has been so pivotal for me that I am going to risk including mentoring material you may feel is not immediately applicable. Imagine with me that the time has come to give directions to those near us, dismiss the crowds around us, and go up on a mountainside to pray. Now let us focus on practical steps toward adopting Jesus' holy habit of prayer retreating.

1. **Set a date:** Yes, even before you know what you will "do" on your retreat, set aside time in your calendar. Mark it booked. Inform your team or friends or family. These spaces are *made*, not *born*. Something else will have to be postponed or cancelled, especially in the beginning. Though it sounds (and may initially feel) like a contradiction, whatever you placed on pause will actually benefit long-term by your absence because you will emerge from the discipline of retreating more clear-minded, creative, and kind. Twenty-four hours is

wonderful, but if an overnight is impossible, set aside a day or an afternoon as a first step.

2. **Reserve a space:** Next, make a reservation for your retreat. Here are a few options:

Monasteries and Catholic solitudes

- Search *monastery + guest rooms + your state* or ask a local Catholic church if there are any monasteries or solitudes in your area.
- Monasteries often have simple guest rooms with a bed, chair, and desk. Many provide vegetarian meals and the opportunity to experience prayer time or vespers in a common chapel.
- Solitudes are more private—often you will not see a soul—but they will be even quieter than monasteries, which may have other guests.
- Most often, these options only request a free-will donation for your stay. At a minimum, try to cover utilities and meals. If possible, give more as a gift for the organization.

A bed-and-breakfast

- Search your area for B&Bs with thick walls to ensure quietness. B&Bs can provide space to rest in comfortable surroundings, fall asleep in a fabulous chair, take a long bath, or enjoy hot tea by a fireplace.
- When I am considering a B&B, I call the owners, explain why I am coming, and ask whether they anticipate that day to be relatively peaceful. Even recently, an honest owner replied, "Oh, we would love to have you come, but that weekend may not be the best for

your purpose. The other rooms are filled with a wedding party."

A friend's house or a hotel

- Perhaps you have a friend with a cabin, a garage apartment, or a restful residence that is empty all day while the family is at work or school. If your friend is happy to give you the keys, be sure to leave their home cleaner than you found it and send a gift card or donation to cover utilities as a thank-you.
- Hotels can also be a good option depending on their noise levels and atmosphere. As with the B&B, ask the manager for a quiet room away from the high school baseball team. Be sure to pray over your room as you begin your time and devote the space to Jesus. Then be wise: unplug the TV and the phone, put away the travel magazines, and visually make the space conducive for prayer and reflection.

3. **Packing to go:** You have chosen the date and made your reservation. Now let us consider how to pack light, physically and emotionally.
   - Pack your favorite Bible, pens, markers, journal, and perhaps a concordance.
   - Carefully select a few books that will nourish your spirit.[1]
   - Consider making the retreat a no-media, low-tech zone.[2]
   - If music tends to be a filler of background noise for you, consider fasting from it for your first few retreats to help you hear the sound of silence.
   - Feel free to bring earplugs, a sound machine, your pillow—the things that help you get a good night's sleep.
   - Look back on chapter 29, guided exercise 5, identifying

your God-print. Then pack a guitar or hiking boots, painting supplies or a fishing pole, quality teas or specialty coffees, whatever would be fun, relaxing, or restful for your soul.[3]

- Tell your closest circle of family and friends about your retreat. Enlist them to help you guard the space.
- Next, we will examine a potential template for shaping the space of your retreat time.

⏸ GUIDED RESPONSE

Thought Focus:

Find a way to take a mini-retreat during your work time today, whether that is in an office or at home. For example, instead of using the time to catch up on social media, take your lunch with Jesus. Or opt for ten minutes of reflective reading instead of crunching in one more to-do on your list. Relax as you rest with God. Be thankful for His constant presence.

Exercise:

In preparation for your twenty-four-hour retreat, set aside one to three hours for a mini-retreat.

1. Look over the suggestions friends offered in chapter 46's research and select a place. For a mini-retreat, consider a safe park, chapel, running trail, library, or art museum. Choose a quiet space that is not your normal hangout. Call ahead to make sure the venue is open and not hosting a local band during your visit.
2. Pack for your time. If you are going to be stationary, bring inspiring pens and a journal, a favorite Bible, and maybe one

book. Even if you are going to be in motion—painting, biking, or running with Jesus—bring a Bible and a journal.

3. If anyone would be worried that you were not instantly available for a few consecutive hours, contact that person and let them know your plans. Then unplug. All the messages will still be waiting for you after the retreat's closing "Amen."

4. Ready? Set? Rest! Start your retreat the moment you leave for it. Keep your head-talk in the plural, e.g., *Jesus, we missed rush-hour traffic, so we should be at the trail within fifteen minutes.*

- When you arrive, read a brief passage from God's Word to meditate on and then reserve space at the end of your time to journal thoughts and impressions.

- As you walk, paint, sit, or run, be honest with Him: tell Him if you feel awkward, distracted, or lost.

- For the moment, shelve any burning questions. As one of my mentors, Sister Rebekka, once said to me, "Seek His Presence, not His provision."

- Plainly talk *with* Him—as opposed to *about* Him—and invest the time as a gift to your Savior.

RETREAT RHYTHMS

Imagine that you have checked in to a monastery, bed-and-breakfast, or guesthouse. Your bags are unpacked, your comfy clothes are on, and you have entered into an expanse of time alone with God. In time, you will establish a rhythm for these sacred spaces of prayer. Here are a few suggestions for a possible starting template from my personal retreats:

Submit your mind to God. Following Jesus with our feet is often easier than following Him with our minds. From the first moments forward, we need to get our heads in the game.

Since breath is among the first gifts we all received, I begin prayer retreats by whispering, "I love You" to Jesus and taking deep, celebratory breaths, each of which reminds me of God's faithful presence. This physical act decelerates my mental motion. As my mind is calmed, I often enjoy a slow walk in the garden, woods, or even just around the room.

With each step, a mind-set is being established: I am not alone, God is not an aloof spectator, and this is a protected space devoted to the nurturing of our relationship. My husband establishes this mind-set with more sweat on his brow. He often begins his retreats with a hike or by working with Jesus outside, clearing paths at our prayer retreat home[1]: same purpose, different methods.

Then I dedicate the next block of time to worship. By nature I am a reflective soul, and journaling or reading would be a more intuitive starting point for me. But over the years, I have found it immeasurably healthier to begin thinking about who God is rather than thinking about who I am or about my current challenges, hurts, and questions.

Occasionally I sing, but more often I worship through Scripture-praise by reading truths about God straight from the Word. This is not intense study. I simply open the Psalms or Gospels and use my voice to speak truth aloud.

Follow repentance with rest. Focusing on God's character almost always guides me safely into repentance. Worship is a purging force. As we mentally magnify God, the revelation we receive of personal sin is clean—condemnation free—because it is overshadowed by God's goodness and grace instead of initiated by perfectionism or a fear-inspired "witch hunt" for error.

When aware of sin, I confess it to God quietly. I may kneel or bow my head and ask for God's forgiveness. Since God reveals to heal, I thank Him for loving me enough to convict me of sin. After waiting in silence for a few minutes to listen and journal, I continue with worship.

Basilea Schlink said, "Jesus and the penitent sinner belong together."[2] She believed that we are never closer to God than when we are asking for His forgiveness because reconciliation was the cause for which Jesus surrendered to crucifixion. These moments of repentance are an integral part of, not a departure from, worship.

Scripture-praising and repentance eventually lead me into a peace-filled pause. Then I often take a nap! I put in my earplugs, snuggle under a blanket, and sleep as long as I can. Fabulous. While falling asleep, I picture God's loving eyes watching over me. These times of rest are holy too. They refresh body and spirit.

I have spent entire retreats simply cycling from worship through repentance into rest and back again. Depending on personality, some may feel the need to emerge from a retreat with something tangible like an answer to a burning prayer or a new teaching. Personally, answers and productivity are not what I hope for from a prayer retreat. Resting with God is the treasure.

Listen and intercede. Worship, repentance, rest, and next, for me, comes a time of listening or waiting. Waiting is a posture of attentiveness. We wait on God because He is worthy of waiting for, whether or not He ever speaks.

In the stillness, I often sense God drawing my attention toward situations and inviting me to partner with Him through intercession. My prayer list is with me at all times, but on a retreat, I wait for God to initiate the intercessory direction. God knows my needs, which comforts me as I leave the needs I deem most pressing at the foot of the cross and follow Him in prayer.

Responding to God's lead, I call on Scripture to pray over issues and areas. Sometimes I write my prayers in a journal or sense specific points of action to implement when I return home. This intercessory emphasis can last a few minutes or fill several hours. Whatever the time frame, there is something perspective inducing in asking God to establish my prayer priorities.

Treasure the final hours. The last minutes of a prayer retreat are precious. I savor them with quietness and a posture of love toward Jesus. I may read a good book, paint a peaceful scene, take a walk with Him, or kneel at a favorite place of prayer. Even as I pack and transition, I work to keep the retreat mind-set: I am not leaving the retreat—the retreat is coming with me. The quietness, trust, forgiveness, and recentered peace do not stay behind as I close a door and drive home.

Like honeysuckle on a windy day, the retreat lingers. Barry always notices increased peace and rest in me when I return. I taste the retreat's fruit in clarity of thought and a noticeable decrease in worry. Years ago, my then four-year-old daughter looked at my retreat-rested face and asked when she could begin taking prayer retreats too.

In addition to these monthly retreats, twice a year I take longer retreats. One is a forty-eight-hour retreat devoted to (1) reviewing the previous year's journals and daily calendar, (2) evaluating the previous year's PI, and (3) transferring words of wisdom, correction, stories for the kids' journals, and ideas for writing from my journal to permanent records. The other extended retreat is a four- to five-day space that is simply devoted to loving Jesus.

When I first started the discipline of prayer retreating, I thought of retreats as a luxury. Now, this Jesus-inspired habit of intentionally investing extended time in loving God and being refreshed by His love is a guarded *given* in my journey. Imagine—oh, imagine!—how the future could be influenced and changed by a generation of leaders and learners whose public presence was anchored in spiritual rest!

⏸ GUIDED RESPONSE

Thought Focus:

Prayerfully meditate on this oft-quoted phrase in its broader context:

This is what the Sovereign LORD, the Holy One of Israel, says:

"In repentance and rest is your salvation,
in quietness and trust is your strength,
but you would have none of it.
You said, 'No, we will flee on horses.'
Therefore you will flee!
You said, 'We will ride off on swift horses.'
Therefore your pursuers will be swift!" (Isaiah 30:15–16)

Exerise:

1. If people want to strengthen their bodies, joining a gym is a great and relatively easy first step. Actually replacing pounds

with muscle takes mental and physical discipline. Recall the last time you began a workout regimen, or interview a friend if you happen to be graced with a crazily high metabolism or an aversion to sweat.

- How did you feel, emotionally and physically, after your first workout? Your second?
- How long did it take for you to see results?
- What thoughts either kept you faithful to the process or led you to abandon the effort?
- What wisdom from that experience can be gleaned to create sober expectations for developing this discipline of prayer retreating?

2. Your first prayer retreat may be filled with revelation and triumphs or maybe not. You may struggle, wondering if anything was accomplished or if you did it right. You may be frustrated that your mind never slowed down or unsure whether or not you could hear God even if He did speak. Such thoughts and questions are normal. The holy habit of prayer retreating becomes more rich and natural over time. If you find yourself wrestling, please remember this: You just gave a no-strings-attached offering to Jesus. He is pleased. Really pleased.

Relax.

Let God measure the fruit.

And make plans for your next retreat.

THE SACRED GO

> When the love of God is indeed my first concern, a deep love for my neighbor can grow. . . .[1]
>
> True contemplatives, then, are not the ones who withdrew from the world to save their own soul, but the ones who enter into the center of the world and pray to God from there.[2]
>
> —HENRI J. M. NOUWEN, *THE GENESEE DIARY: REPORT FROM A TRAPPIST MONASTERY*

WHAT YOU WILL NEED FOR THE EXERCISES

✔ Your Personal Inventory
✔ A notepad *or* journal
✔ Your Life Scroll
✔ A fine-point permanent marker

THE OVERFLOW

In this final movement, we come full circle and consider once again the story of the original Sacred Slow. Though the nation as a whole rejected God's call to honor a Sabbath Year until after the Exile, surely several souls still risked obedience.

One here, two there, leading their families and villages against an ancient error that—to this day—equates visible increase with God's favor and visible decrease with man's failure.

I wonder what effect these Sabbath Year risk-takers might have had on their watching world: on anxious neighbors, bitter brothers, skeptical sisters, and impressionable children.

After all, saturated souls water others by their very presence.

Surely this was the dramatic drawing power of Jesus as He walked in continuous communion with the Father here on earth.

Jesus' public speech was the overflow of sacred silence.

Jesus' outward acts were the overflow of internal stillness.

Jesus' physical steps were the overflow of spiritual rest.

And Jesus' suffering was the overflow of disciplined love.

Jesus' saturated soul gave hope to the sincerely thirsty and offended the satisfied dry.

Our saturated souls can, and will, do the same. Because intimacy with God can, and will, overflow to water a waiting world.

God-consciousness tames and trains self-consciousness. This Sacred Slow pursuit of continuous attentiveness to God enables us to be true to self but not suffocated by self. Every single moment invested in spiritual intentionality expands our capacity to receive and return God's love. And *living loved* frees us to love others.

Jesus' response to the woman caught in adultery beautifully illustrates the power of such continuous attentiveness to Father God. Like water poured over a fire, Jesus' generous authority extinguished the accusations of the leaders' stingy self-righteousness. In the resulting smoke, Jesus' presence graced a soul with hope, healing, and a call to holiness:

> "Woman, where are they? Has no one condemned you?"
>
> "No one, sir," she said.
>
> "Then neither do I condemn you," Jesus declared. "Go now and leave your life of sin." (John 8:10–11)

Jesus was silent when the leaders wanted Him to speak. When He did speak, no doubt they wished He had remained silent. With a calmness that only manifests in the souls of those who know God is with them, Jesus stood between stones and a sinner. As He wrote in the dirt from which He had formed us, Jesus' presence preached a sermon too powerful for words. Yes, the woman had been caught in the act of adultery. And the leaders had been caught in the deception of hypocrisy. Grace silenced the latter and saved the former. In the moving words of Howard Thurman,

> He met the woman where she was, and he treated her as if she were already where she now willed to be. In dealing with her, he "believed" her into the fulfillment of her possibilities. He stirred her confidence into activity. He placed a crown over her head which for the rest of her life she would keep trying to grow tall enough to wear.[1]

This is what intimacy with God does! Such a life multiplies faith by simply being faithful. Though we are yet infants in our shared pursuit of practicing the presence of God, every step we make is fragranced with a grace that lifts the eyes and heads of those around us upward to their King.

So I think of you, my friend, of your life multiplied, and my eyes fill with tears. I consider the overflow of your Sacred Slow journey and its repercussions in unseen realms, and I feel great joy.

Yes, we all have further to go, but we cannot allow what is left to incite us to underestimate what is gained. You have risked attending to the interior, and that work is to be celebrated.

⏸ GUIDED RESPONSE

Thought Focus:

What effect has your holy departure from Fast Faith had on others so far? Journal your response and savor this final movement of *The Sacred Slow*.

Exercise:

1. As we near the end of *The Sacred Slow*, return to the Personal Inventory you developed in movement two. Since it was created with God through listening prayer, it will now be evaluated with God through listening prayer.
   - Schedule thirty to sixty minutes at your favorite thinking spot with your favorite coffee and favorite pen and journal. This is all celebration!
   - Whether you have reread your PI periodically or have not touched it since its creation, open it symbolically before God as an offering. Through scripture meditation or

song, quiet your mind with God and ask Him to grant you His perspective.

- Consider the season theme and area applications line by line with this prayer in mind: "God, from Your perspective, was there *movement*?" This is a distinctly different query than, "Was there achievement?" When my youngest first attempted to stand and promptly fell on his diaper-padded backside, our whole family burst into applause. We did not withhold our affirmation until he "succeeded." We had a party because *standing* was in his heart. It is critical in evaluating an inventory that we allow God to be the good parent He actually is and not project on Him any achievement-oriented perfectionism that may be loitering about in our souls.

- After celebrating movement, ask God what form intentionality should take in your next season. You may adapt this template or utilize an entirely different tool. But I encourage you to continue finding a vessel to carry spiritual intentionality into your future.

2. Then share the celebration with a friend for personal accountability and the strengthening of community.

OPEN EYES

We examined these bookends in chapter 19:

> The job description in Mark 3 and the Great Commission in Matthew 28 bookend and mirror each other. They contain the same elements in reverse. In Mark 3, Jesus spoke of being with Him, being sent out to preach, and having authority. In Matthew 28, Jesus spoke of having authority, then described their role as sent ones, and ended with a promise of presence.

Jesus desires our witness *of* Him to be the directed overflow of nearness *to* Him. However, nearness does not automate witness. Fruit, in any millennia, must be cultivated.

Consider the disciples who were called to be with Jesus. They walked with Him and talked with Him and proceeded to walk by others without saying a word.

Remember the Samaritan woman who spent time alone with Jesus by a well and then brought her whole town to meet Him? Nearness with Jesus immediately produced the fruit of proclamation in her life. However, she was not the first person familiar with Jesus' presence to go into town that day.

The disciples had been there earlier.

We read in John 4:8, "His disciples had gone into the town to buy food." In town, they interacted with bakers, fishermen, and fruit sellers in the marketplace long enough to buy sufficient food to feed at least thirteen.

So twelve leaders who walked alongside Jesus 24/7 went into a town and said, "We'd like to buy six fish and a loaf of bread." How many people followed them back to meet Jesus?

Not even one.

One Samaritan woman who had spent perhaps less than an hour with Jesus went into the same town and said, "Come, see a man who told me everything I ever did. Could this be the Messiah?" (John 4:29). How many people followed her back to meet Jesus?

Exactly. The whole town!

Perhaps the Twelve felt they were not "on duty" in town. After all, they were shopping, not serving or speaking at one of Jesus' designated outreaches. Whatever the reasoning, Jesus' call to them was clear: "I tell you, open your eyes and look at the fields! They are ripe for harvest" (v. 35).

As the disciples strained their brains to look beyond their appetites, agendas, and prejudices in the direction Jesus indicated, imagine what they must have seen: not wheat wagging in the wind but an entire town just trying to find their way to Jesus.

The disciples walked with Jesus closely but still viewed evangelism as an event.

In the enormous chunk of life that existed outside of outreaches, they lived attached to Jesus and detached from the lost.

My God, open our eyes.

Christ has no body now on earth but yours; no hands but yours; no feet but yours.

Yours are the eyes through which the compassion of Christ must look out on the world.

Yours are the feet with which He is to go about doing good.

Yours are the hands with which He is to bless His people.

—TERESA OF AVILA[1]

⏸ GUIDED RESPONSE

Thought Focus:

Today, simply ask the Lord of the harvest to help you live with open eyes.

Exercise:

After Jesus' ascension and the day of Pentecost, we see evidence that the disciples learned from Jesus' sploshy example and began to live with open eyes. They saw a beggar on their way to the temple (Acts 3:1–8). They paused to give guidance to an Ethiopian on the road (8:26–39). They waited around after a dramatic rescue to witness to a desperate jailer (16:25–34).

As we walk intentionally with Jesus, let us seek to manifest His love to every soul we encounter: Christ cannot be segregated from His cause.

1. Nearness with God does not mean that we sing "Amazing Grace" at gas stations or read the Bible aloud at grocery stores. It means that we listen to God while we live in this world. Recall the faces or voices you encountered within the last twenty-four hours. With God, remember whether you saw them as jobs or souls. Did you notice their eyes or their clothes? Ask God to help you remember them as He does.

2. Over the next two days, as you interact with the customer-service rep on the phone, the neighborhood child selling cookies, the clerk behind the counter, and the coworker asking for your input, say to yourself, *My Jesus died for this soul.*

3. As you go into town to buy food, pray John 3:16 silently over your city's bakers, fishermen, and fruit sellers. As you walk your neighborhood or work in the office, pray: *My God, You so loved these souls that You gave Your only Son. May this man/woman/child believe in You and have eternal life.*

4. Ask Jesus to reveal ways in which your intimacy with Him can overflow to water other souls. You entered *The Sacred Slow* to transition from surge-to-surge, feast or famine, Fast Faith into moment-by-moment, intentional nearness with God. May such a shift be felt by the waiting world!

YOU+

You may, or may not, have wondered what prompted me to create *The Sacred Slow*. As we are nearing the conclusion of this journey together, perhaps it is time to supply the why.

> In short: you.
> Yes, you.

I may never have the privilege of shaking your hand or of hearing your voice, but you are still the why.

> More accurately: you+.

The plus is the wild exponential factor of faith. The plus is the promise of non-aloneness. Two lines connect to become a universal symbol for add, increase, and grow.

You+ means that spiritual intentionality will bear fruit in you and through you.

You+ means that your life, your peace, and your spiritual DNA will naturally prompt others to ask you how to walk more closely with God.

You+ means that whatever you have received from the Sacred Slow journey will be passed on to others for the love of God.

Call it mentoring, coaching, discipling, the guy tribe, or Seventh

Year sisters. Implement it in a life group, office, church, family, or neighborhood. But my hope is that you will invite others to join you in practicing the presence of God.

By God's great mercy and His generous gifts of outstanding mentors, I began intentionally guiding others into spiritual health more than thirty years ago. I remember asking one of my earliest mentors, "Donna, you are entrusting your mentoring group to me. Aren't you nervous?" She replied, "Nervous? I'm scared to death. But I'm convinced that this practice of shared life is biblical, and that is where I place my hope."

Share the *life*.

Life is not the offspring of paper or programs. Life is always the offspring of life. If *The Sacred Slow* has been fruitful, it is not because letters have been carefully arranged on a page, but because the principles these letters carry have been sown into a *life*, yours.

Share the *life*.

And while you wait for the fruit to grow, see the future by faith.

See a future where leaders live led.

See a future where learners live loved.

See a future where authority with others is the overflow of proximity with God.

See the lost observing well-watered souls and noting that they have been with Jesus.

See healthy churches unscarred by exhausted pastors' failures and driven boards' agendas.

See marketplace ministers immune to people's praise and attuned to God's whispers.

See.

Sow.

Wait.

Grow.

You

+

+

+

+

⏸ GUIDED RESPONSE

Thought Focus:

And the things you have heard me say in the presence of many witnesses entrust to reliable people who will also be qualified to teach others. (2 Timothy 2:2)

Consider the four generations represented in Paul's admonition: Paul → Timothy and the many witnesses who also heard Paul → reliable people qualified to teach → others.

Prayerfully take an action step toward entrusting what you have received from God in your Sacred Slow journey to the next generation.

Exercise:

If you stand on a sidewalk with a tray of food, several curious strangers may ask what you are doing, and one or two brave souls may even take a bite. With the time-tested exception of pizza in a college dorm, good food does not create a party. However, if you bring good food to a party already in existence, it is gobbled up in community. In the words of my friend Charity Reeb, "Find the party."

Think of groups already gathering in the marketplace, neighborhood, and church that would benefit from the spiritual principles and practices you are now seeking to implement. If no groups come to mind, start your own.

1. Write down potential groups (i.e., parties). For example, perhaps your church's life groups would benefit from reading *Practicing His Presence* (by Brother Lawrence and Frank Laubach) to connect each member in a common pursuit of nearness with God. Or a morning prayer group might be encouraged on the job by the "God in the room" principle from chapter 12. Or some of your friends may truly enjoy going with you on a prayer retreat.

2. Pray for these groups and listen for God's direction.

3. Offer to share or teach from your experience:
   - Write a blog or article for a website or newsletter about the power of intentionality.
   - Post quotes on what you are learning in your journey.
   - Have coffee with a group leader and share your favorite reading or journal entry.
   - Lead others through a repeat of *The Sacred Slow*.
   - Offer to share a brief devotional with a prayer group about your holy departure from Fast Faith.
   - In other words, share the love. As Jesus said, "Freely you have received; freely give" (Matthew 10:8).

ANTICIPATION

My first sabbatical concluded the same way it commenced at the same desert prayer retreat center in Arizona. Hour upon hour, I sat surrounded by sand waiting for closure. Surely someone would tap me on the shoulder with a special scripture or strong encouragement. Perhaps God would gift me with a closing insight or new song. Maybe a book would fall open to an astounding passage or a lost note would be found in my journal.

As the hours turned into days, a closing punctuation mark to my experience never came. Far from being the end, I realized that the sabbatical announced a new beginning. I sensed God saying, *Child, you are the only one waiting for closure. I didn't call you to take some time off. I called you into a different way of living.*

In the same way, a Sacred Slow does not end. It simply evolves into a Sacred Go:

- Go with God into all the world.
- Treasure rest as a prerequisite to fruitfulness.
- Befriend pain as an ally of love.
- Steward time as a gift.
- Discipline your strengths to submit to His timing.
- Believe that God designed you to know and enjoy Him.
- Ground yourself with the glorious tension of God's Word.
- Live with Jesus at the center and His presence as your home.

- Align your self-thoughts with God's gracious thoughts.
- Nurture your God-concept with honesty and honor for the Scriptures.
- Intend to attend to God's presence.
- Listen well to God. Love well through God. And live *well loved* by God.

These twelve movements of *The Sacred Slow* have all worked toward a common goal. In the words of John of the Cross:

> At the evening of life, you will be examined in love.
> Learn to love as God desires to be loved.[1]

Intimacy with God builds layer upon layer. Developed disciplines, realized repentance, and learned lessons fuse with delayed dreams, ongoing challenges, and unanswered questions into a path on which we walk by faith, not by sight, with Jesus into the next season.

Anticipate what that season will hold!

Mystery? Probably. And within that mystery, ever deeper dimensions of love for God.

As you turn the final page of *The Sacred Slow*, I leave you with a glorious thought from the pen of Frank Laubach:

> I feel convinced that for me, and for you who read, there lie ahead undiscovered continents of spiritual living compared with which we are infants in arms.[2]

⏸ GUIDED RESPONSE

Thought Focus:
Recall your responses to the thought foci of chapters 1 through 6.

Remember your life-as-a-movie analogy, and dream with God about a sequel as you begin a new season of spiritual life.

Exercise:

With anticipation in your heart, rest in God's continuous presence. Exercise the discipline of gratitude by thanking Him specifically for both the "developed disciplines, realized repentance, learned lessons" and the "delayed dreams, ongoing challenges, and unanswered questions" of your Sacred Slow journey.

1. Select a few of these points of thanksgiving to celebrate with a good friend.
2. Reflect on your life since beginning *The Sacred Slow*. Unfold your Life Scroll and, row by row, make any additions that you feel are significant.
   - Row 1: Events that the government and insurance company know about
   - Row 2: Significant moments in your journey with Jesus
   - Row 3: Moments of joy
   - Row 4: Moments of pain
   - Row 5: Adjectives that capture your self-perception
   - Row 6: Adjectives that capture your view of God
3. In conversation with God, record your observations or impressions about these additions in row 7.
4. Now dream with Jesus. Set aside a morning or take a prayer retreat to simply say, "Thank You." Wait on Him as a love offering. Listen whether or not anything is heard. Such a gift honors our Savior in a world that so often rejects Him. Our first ministry has always been to love Him.

May our collective love refresh His heart.

[TOOLBOX]

TWELVE-WEEK FACILITATOR GUIDE

The twelve movements of *The Sacred Slow* build on one another. Each chapter's content flow is extremely intentional. As a facilitator, you have five responsibilities:

1. Create space to fully engage in the readings, thought foci, and exercises.
2. Select a handful of questions from the more-than-you-need lists below.
3. Ask these questions in an atmosphere that encourages honesty and content integration.
4. Calmly refuse to fix or prematurely dismiss difficult questions that arise.
5. Close the group time in prayer for the participants.

In other words, asking questions—not imparting answers—is your goal. The un-done-ness of the fifty-two experiences is intentional and essential. Too often we tie up Bible lessons with a neat bow when real life is anything but tidy and tame. Along with your group, experience the journey, be honest about your own un-done-ness, and anticipate the fruit of a more sustainable and satisfying nearness with God based on His presence, not your performance.

MOVEMENT/WEEK ONE:
TWO STORIES

	READING SUMMARY	EXERCISE EMPHASIS
Intro	Overview of book's purpose and content	None
1	Explanation of Fast Faith	Gather a team. Fill in Life Scroll row 1 with your timeline.
2	Explanation of the Sacred Slow	Fill in Life Scroll row 2 with spiritually formative moments.
3	The number seven (symbolic of rest) and introductory study of the Sabbath (Seventh) Year	Fill in Life Scroll rows 3 and 4 with joyous and painful moments.
4	The substance of the Seventh Year	Fill in Life Scroll row 5 with your self-concepts.
5	The challenge and cost for the Israelites of neglecting the biblical Sabbath Year	Fill in Life Scroll row 6 with your God-concepts.

Optional Supplementary Resources

Anonymous: Jesus' Hidden Years . . . and Yours by Alicia
    Britt Chole
"The Sabbath Year," an academic essay by Alicia Britt Chole

Optional Memory Verses

All the days ordained for me were written in your book
    before one of them came to be. (Psalm 139:16)
[The LORD said . . .] "But in the seventh year the land is
    to have a year of sabbath rest, a sabbath to the LORD."
    (Leviticus 25:1, 4)

[The Lord said . . .] "Everything under heaven belongs to
me." (Job 41:11)
Never will I leave you; never will I forsake you. (Hebrews 13:5)

Chapter-by-Chapter Facilitator Notes

The Life Scroll is among the most healing and insight-producing
exercises for those I mentor. Some exercises may be emotionally challenging. But in row 7, as participants step back and begin mixing layers,
their histories are often infused with new meaning and connections.

Additionally, the exercises in this first movement may press on
some wounds that need further healing. Prepare a short list of trusted
Christian counselors and therapists in your region that specialize in
areas of grief, abuse, marital conflict, and freedom from shame.

[1] The Life Scroll can be found in the Toolbox in the back
     of the book. Though at times a heart-head-hands intensive,
     this exercise will enrich the entire experience by gifting each
     participant with self-awareness of their history and increased
     sensitivity to God's breath over their days.

[2] Departing from Fast Faith is not a rejection of the rich
     resources available in our day. But it does reframe these
     resources as helps instead of hopes. God is with us and He
     is our hope. This means that every moment for every Jesus-
     follower around the world can be filled with nearness with
     God. That nearness is not awaiting music. It is the fruit of
     attentiveness. Encourage participants to reposition—not
     abandon—their favorite tools and boosts.

[3] Some may wonder about the emphasis on the number seven.
     Honestly, I avoided number studies for a very long time
     because some felt a wee bit flaky for my logic-loving mind.
     But seven is clearly symbolic of rest, and this study will lead

into an examination of the biblical seventh year. Speak of seven as a reminder to rest, and ask participants to evaluate how rested they truly are in body, mind, and soul.

[4] Occasionally a participant feels driven to find a modern parallel application to the biblical Sabbath Year such as cancelling debts, giving generously, or quitting their job for a year. Though we certainly do not want to hinder how God may be speaking, encourage the group to commit potential applications to prayer. Sometimes we act so quickly that the water of the Word does not have time to penetrate to depths that produce lasting (as opposed to immediate but short-lived) change.

[5] This is a real story about real people. Encourage the group to take the story off of any flannel graph in their minds and place themselves in the text. Draw on world events and discuss the realities of exile. Discuss the costs of both obedience and disobedience.

Chapter-by-Chapter Discussion Guide

Introduction

Reading:
- Alicia mentions three certainties supporting every line of *The Sacred Slow*. Which of these three speak to you the most?
- Why do you think Alicia places such emphasis on your responsibility to be honest?

[1] What Is Fast Faith?

Reading:
- As you begin this fifty-two-experience investment in your spiritual health, what thoughts, concerns, or questions do

you have regarding what this journey may (or may not) hold for you?

- In your own words, what is Fast Faith?

Thought Focus: Share one of the sets you selected for your life as a movie.

Exercise: Did you find it challenging or easy, comfortable or stressful, to fill in your timeline with the events that the government and your insurance company know about?

[2] What Is the Sacred Slow?

Reading:

- How naturally comfortable are you with being "undone"?
- What was the "more direct route" spoken of by Brother Lawrence?

Thought Focus: Share one spiritual formation scene that your life as a movie could not omit.

Exercise: Was it easy or difficult to identify spiritually formative moments/events in your Life Scroll? How many of these moments were outside of your control?

[3] The Number of Rest

Reading:

- Seven in Scripture speaks of "intentional times," "set-apart spaces," "waiting, warring, warning, and wisdom." How will you set apart the space you need to enter fully into this Sacred Slow experience?
- Numbers carried more weight in ancient times than they seem to today. Consider Anna becoming a widow in the

seventh year of her marriage (Luke 2:36–38). How might widowhood have been perceived in her culture?
- Reflect on how Anna's response to her seventh year ultimately positioned her to see the Messiah.

Thought Focus: Share one high or low from your life-as-a-movie trailer.

Exercise: Was it easier to identify moments of joy or moments of pain? Apply your responses to your daily life. What do you find yourself reflecting on more at the end of each day—moments of pain or moments of joy?

[4] The Original Sacred Slow

Reading:
- In what ways might honoring God's commanded Sabbath/ seventh year have "drastically changed the fabric of a community" (page 18)?
- How costly might such a year of rest have been to the original hearers?
- "Rest the land and hear the Law . . . release indentured servants and cancel debts . . . make no profit and give generously" (page 18). Which of these emphases stands out to you? Why?

Thought Focus: What qualities would you need to characterize any actor who played you in your life as a movie?

Exercise: Did any of your Life Scroll self-perceptions surprise you?

[5] God's Issue with Clenched Fists

Reading:
- "God does seem to consistently take issue with clenched fists" (page 21). Share any thoughts you had as you read these words.

- In what ways do you feel you are living "an open-handed existence" (page 22)?
- Respond to the final question of the reading: "What could have been avoided—let alone gained—if the community had embraced the space?" (page 23).

Thought Focus: Where was God in one (or more) of the scenes of your life as a movie?

Exercise: How easy or difficult was it to give yourself permission to be fully honest in this exercise?

MOVEMENT/WEEK TWO: ADDING INTENTIONALITY

	READING SUMMARY	EXERCISE EMPHASIS
6	Revealing the symptoms and danger of refusing to listen to God	Fill in Life Scroll row 7 by mixing layers to reveal new correlations in our stories.
7	Listening as a spiritual discipline and the power of silence	Create your Personal Inventory. Listen heaven-down for God's direction for your lives.
8	The need to hear and heed God's voice	Develop your Personal Inventory. Prayerfully identify application responses to the heaven-down theme.
9	The relationship between spiritual passivity and fruitlessness	Finalize your Personal Inventory. Incorporate feedback from friends.

Optional Supplementary Resources

Mansions of the Heart: Exploring the Seven Stages of Spiritual Growth by R. Thomas Ashbrook

Optional Memory Verses

The Sovereign LORD . . . wakens my ear to listen like one
    being instructed. The Sovereign LORD has opened
    my ears; I have not been rebellious, I have not turned
    away. (Isaiah 50:4–5)

"For I know the plans I have for you," declares the LORD.
    (Jeremiah 29:11)

Consider carefully what you hear. . . . With the measure
    you use, it will be measured to you—and even more.
    (Mark 4:24)

Others, like seed sown on good soil, hear the word, accept
    it, and produce a crop—some thirty, some sixty, some
    a hundred times what was sown. (Mark 4:20)

Chapter-by-Chapter Facilitator Notes

[6] As a facilitator, work to make the why and what of "not
listening" evident. What can it look like? What do we experience internally when someone does not listen to us? What
does it feel like when we choose not to listen to others? How
do we justify not listening in our relationships?

[7] Listening is valuable whether or not the listener hears God's
voice. Listening cultivates a spiritual attentiveness that posi-
tions our soul for nearness with God and strengthens our
will to discipline our minds. In other words, the action is
more powerful than any answer we might hear.

[8] As a facilitator, share a personal example from childhood or
adulthood when you experienced a gap between hearing and
heeding. As a group, brainstorm ways you can all strengthen
your wills to heed.

[9] The Personal Inventory is a real-time application of the

reading's emphasis on listening. Unlike a self-improvement list, PI's begin heaven-down by waiting on God. Listening does not have to be overly mystical. The Scriptures are our primary source for God's voice.

Chapter-by-Chapter Discussion Guide

[6] The Underestimated Danger of Not Listening

Reading:
- Consider the much-loved Jeremiah 29:11–13 in context. How might the original hearers' usage of this passage differ from ours today?
- Summarize Alicia's definitions of *listening* and *not listening*.
- How did not listening lead Jeremiah's generation into idolatry? How might not listening lead us into idolatry today?

Thought Focus: Share any differences you have discerned between God's review and your review of your life as a movie.

Exercise: Toward the end of *The Sacred Slow*, you will be referencing your Life Scroll once more. Until then, what is currently your top take-home from this exercise?

[7] A Curious Remedy for Idolatry

Reading:
- Alicia calls *listening* a spiritual discipline. What is the difference between being a skilled listener and simply being in proximity?
- Is silence soothing or stressful for you? What emotions do you experience when silence is extended?
- How can silence be a "purging force"?

Thought Focus: Share your in-process purpose statement for this season of your life.

Exercise: What was it like to approach the Personal Inventory "heaven-down" by listening for God's guidance instead of "earth-up" by listing everything in life that you would like to change?

[8] The Sound of Listening

Reading:
- What thoughts or feelings arise within you when someone talks about listening to/for God?
- Pause in silence for a moment to identify, in as much detail as possible, everything you currently can hear.
- It is hard to listen on the run. Listening requires a pause. In our noisy, motion-addicted world, what will it take to create such a pause in your life?
- Like Eve, why do we stand "close enough to forbidden fruit for Satan to use it as a speaking prop"?

Thought Focus: How would you personally answer the question, "Why do I exist?"

Exercise: Alicia emphasizes thinking with God as opposed to brainstorming solo. How easy or hard was it to "press your mind to stay in conversation with God" throughout this exercise?

[9] Seed #3 and the Enemy's Plan B

Reading:
- Rephrase what Alicia refers to as Satan's plan A and plan B.
- Reread Mark 4:20. What three verbs distinguish the fourth seed?

- Think about those you interact with daily. How might they benefit from your commitment to hear and heed God's voice?

Thought Focus: Share one of the action steps you identified toward adding intentionality to your spiritual journey.

Exercise: Alicia states, "Our growth is better watered by meditating on who He is than by obsessing over who we are not." Since the PI process began heaven-down, discuss ways to keep the PI a response to God's initiative instead of one more item on a to-do list.

MOVEMENT/WEEK THREE: GOD-CONCEPTS

	READING SUMMARY	EXERCISE EMPHASIS
10	The danger of spiritual misthink	Fill in the blank: God, I think You are _____.
11	Doing nothing as a choice	Ask, "What am I thinking about God now?"
12	The presence and power of God in the room	Interview close friends about your God-concept.
13	Learning to think backward to discover the source of our God-concepts	Compare portraits from chapters 10, 11, and 12.

Optional Supplementary Resources

Knowledge of the Holy by A. W. Tozer

Jesus Manifesto: Restoring the Supremacy and Sovereignty of Jesus Christ by Leonard Sweet and Frank Viola

Optional Memory Verses

[Jesus asked,] "Who do you say I am?" Simon Peter answered, "You are the Messiah, the Son of the living God." (Matthew 16:15–16)

The compassionate and gracious God, slow to anger, abounding in love and faithfulness . . . forgiving wickedness, rebellion and sin. Yet he does not leave the guilty unpunished. (Exodus 34:6–7)

And surely I am with you always, to the very end of the age. (Matthew 28:20)

You will keep in perfect peace those whose minds are steadfast, because they trust in you. (Isaiah 26:3)

Chapter-by-Chapter Facilitator Notes

This movement guides participants through the process of seeing and then editing their God canvases. Expect intense interaction in this and the next movement. Nothing is deeper than our God-concepts and self-concepts. God is already aware of our distortions and misthink. He only reveals to heal.

[10] I cannot overemphasize the importance of this exercise. Encourage participants to take the "God, I think You are . . ." exercise with them and invest time in creating a God-concept canvas that reflects their honest views. Accurate acknowledgement is a giant step toward increased health.

[11] The question may arise, "Isn't reading the Bible enough?" The Word is essential, but too often we go passive after we close the Book. As a facilitator, pray for your group to actively resist spiritual passivity and to rise up to reclaim an accurate and awesome view of God.

[12] Some may sincerely have trouble attempting to process the concept of God in the room. Assure them that such a challenge is normal. The goal is to awaken to the reality that God is *with* us as a step toward a lifestyle of consciously acknowledging God's actual presence in every moment. Also, inviting others to weigh in on various exercises can be uncomfortable. Remind the group to choose the interviewees wisely, i.e., ask healthy people who will not abuse the invitation. These exercises keep spiritual introspection connected to community and real-world application.

[13] The discipline of thinking backward is a mighty tool for spiritual formation. It may be helpful to walk through a few fictional scenarios as a group to illustrate this discipline. For example, what thoughts or beliefs could prompt an employer to shame an employee in front of his or her peers?

Chapter-by-Chapter Discussion Guide

[10] The Source of Spiritual Misthink

Reading:
- To date, how much energy do you feel you have invested in "identifying, purifying, and enriching [your] God-concept"?
- Review Tozer's quotes. How might a "right belief about God" relieve you of "temporal problems"?
- What do you think Alicia means when she says, "The Word heard is not enough"? Do you agree/disagree? Why?

Thought Focus: Were there any responses that you hesitated to write down? Why?

Exercise: Did anything surprise or encourage you about this first God-concept portrait?

[11] How to Water Thorns

Reading:

- Alicia explains, "I nurtured the thorn trees by omission. When I first saw them, I decided to do *nothing*. And doing nothing is a choice." To consider this concept more concretely, discuss the impact of passivity on a yard or garden.
- What thorns are currently threatening your fruitfulness?
- A continuous point of concern is how students sometimes spiritually flounder in college. How might the thorns of misthink about God's character contribute to their vulnerability?

Thought Focus: What thorns in your God-concept are you becoming aware of?

Exercise: Share any fresh insights about your God-concept from this second God-concept portrait.

[12] God in the Room

Reading:

- Share any responses you had to the story of the woman who had not seen God in the room of her pain.
- Are you currently aware of any discrepancies between your official and working God-concepts?
- Which of the closing thoughts on the power of "God in the room" mean the most to you today?

Thought Focus: Share any discoveries you made this week about God in the room.

Exercise: Creating this third God-concept portrait was a risky and vulnerable exercise! What thoughts from those you interviewed did you find comforting? Concerning?

[13] Thinking Backward

Reading:

- Read Isaiah 26:3–4 and John 14:27. Contrast the world's peace with Jesus' peace.
- Alicia views our attitudes and behaviors as fruit of our underlying thoughts and beliefs. Do you agree or disagree?
- Though thinking backward is strenuous, as a discipline it can be a game-changer! Are there areas in your life where thinking backward would actually help you move forward spiritually?

Thought Focus: Share any insights you discovered from thinking backward this week.

Exercise: What are the greatest areas of strength in your God-concept? Did anything puzzle you as you contrasted the three different canvases? What attributes of God need further attention in your life?

MOVEMENT/WEEK FOUR: SELF-CONCEPTS

	READING SUMMARY	EXERCISE EMPHASIS
14	How we mentally poison ourselves	What do you say to yourself about yourself?
15	True intellectual strength	Request input from trusted friends.
16	Revoking all-access passes into our minds	Address your self-thoughts.
17	The challenge of changing locks in our minds	Use scripture as an antidote to toxic thinking.

Optional Supplementary Resources

Search for Significance: Seeing Your True Worth Through God's Eyes by Robert McGee

Optional Memory Verses

May these words of my mouth and this meditation of my heart be pleasing in your sight, LORD, my Rock and my Redeemer. (Psalm 19:14)

If anything is excellent or praiseworthy—think about such things. (Philippians 4:8b)

Above all else, guard your heart, for everything you do flows from it. (Proverbs 4:23)

We take captive every thought to make it obedient to Christ. (2 Corinthians 10:5b)

Chapter-by-Chapter Facilitator Notes

[14] And now we are getting personal. God-concept always affects self-concept. Remind the group of "God in the room" in this process. It can be easy for participants to disconnect negative self-talk from God's loving call for them to see themselves through His redeeming eyes.

[15] At times we treat our minds more like trash cans than treasures and welcome without scrutiny whatever the world throws our way. Guide your group in brainstorming a working definition of spiritual formation. Odds are that something holistic will emerge, leaving no area off limits to God's redeeming work.

[16] Participants may get stuck trying to identify what thoughts should be let into their thought space. Encourage them to focus less on specific thoughts and more on developing the

discipline of pausing. A short prayerful pause in which we whisper, *Jesus, can You and I think this thought together?* can drastically change our thinking patterns.

[17] A relevant discussion topic could be to consider the church's understanding of pride and humility. Does humility mean that we amplify our weaknesses? Is it prideful to think well of ourselves? Misthink in this area often contributes to a false but felt belief that meditation on untruth has benefits.

Chapter-by-Chapter Discussion Guide

[14] Does God Have an Opinion?

Reading:

- What could motivate someone to self-abuse by mental self-poisoning?
- Do you think that God has an opinion about your self-thoughts?
- *The Sacred Slow* content has often been described as surgical. At 25 percent of the way into your journey, share how the experience is shaping you.

Thought Focus: Overall, do you feel that you were kind or harsh to yourself in this exercise? If harsh, did you ever find yourself reasoning, "Yeah, but it's still kinder than I deserve" or ". . . than what [insert a name] would say about me"?

Exercise: Growing up, was it more acceptable in your culture to say positive or negative things about yourself? Share any family or cultural beliefs that may have contributed to this environment.

[15] Sorting the Mail

Reading:

- Have you ever been in an environment hostile to your faith? If so, in what ways did the challenge affect you?
- Respond to Alicia's statement: "True intellectual strength is not merely the ability *to* think. It is the ability *to choose* what to think and when to think."
- By nature, do you sort the mail in your mind? If so, share some strategies you implement. If not, how do you feel this practice might be beneficial in this specific season of your life?

Thought Focus: How easy or hard was it for you to sort the mail?

Exercise: How did you feel about inviting others into your formation process? What reasons do you think Alicia might have for calling you to take these steps?

[16] New Rules, New Start

Reading:

- Recall the three reasons the generous soul welcomed all into her home. Do any of these reasons feel familiar?
- After changing the locks, the generous soul said, "It would have been easier to leave everything the way it was." Why is taking the path of least resistance so very, very attractive?
- Share any ways in which you sense God calling you to increase vigilance in your mind.

Thought Focus: How did it feel to think of every thought as a guest?

Exercise: In what ways has the Holy Spirit historically brought His concerns to your attention? For example, have you sensed God's conviction through quiet impressions, Scripture, sermons, a child's insight, or lessons from nature?

[17] Changing the Locks

Reading:

- How would you describe your thought-life's current level of security?
- Do you agree with Alicia's belief that there's "fear in the Enemy's eyes that we are even having this discussion"? Why or why not?
- Which of the three weapons Alicia mentions seems the most practical for you? Share any other strategies you may personally use.

Thought Focus: What "perceived benefits" may have contributed to the overdue status of your identified lock change?

Exercise: Share any scriptures that have become more meaningful to you in this journey toward a healthier thought-life.

MOVEMENT/WEEK FIVE: CENTRALIZING HIS PRESENCE

	READING SUMMARY	EXERCISE EMPHASIS
18	Living life as a duet instead of a solo	Think about God as your center.
19	Being with Jesus is still a literal calling	Interview those who walk closely with God.
20	Christ is in us (but not us)	Practice God's presence in your daily life.
21	The power of praying Scripture over yourself	Craft an inheritance prayer.

Optional Supplementary Resources

Practicing His Presence by Brother Lawrence and Frank Laubach
The Praying Plumber of Lisburn: A Sketch of God's Dealings with Thomas Haire by A. W. Tozer

Optional Memory Verses

The LORD would speak to Moses face to face, as one speaks to a friend. (Exodus 33:11)

He appointed twelve that they might be with him and that he might send them out to preach and to have authority to drive out demons. (Mark 3:14–15)

To them God has chosen to make known among the Gentiles the glorious riches of this mystery, which is Christ in you, the hope of glory. (Colossians 1:27)

For we are God's handiwork, created in Christ Jesus to do good works, which God prepared in advance for us to do. (Ephesians 2:10)

Chapter-by-Chapter Facilitator Notes

All four readings are designed to transition participants away from living alone in their heads and toward continuous conversation with God. This movement is the heartbeat of *The Sacred Slow*. Savor it and urge participants to explore means of retraining their minds to "live in the plural" with God. Some may feel discouraged with their attempts. Remind them of how we cheer a baby's first steps even though it often ends with a fall. We cheer because standing is in the child's heart. How much more must our heavenly Father cheer us all on in these first steps toward more sustainable intimacy with Him!

[18] Some may wonder if practicing God's presence is a reality reserved for certain personalities. But every personality will find some disciplines easier and some harder. Invite the group to help one another see ways in which their unique wirings can be an asset to this pursuit.

[19] Permit queries that may be rarely verbalized such as, *How do we really know that He is with us?* or *If God is present and powerful, why don't I feel His presence?* Compare God's presence to the wind that cannot be seen or to the sun that cannot always be felt.

[20] Focus on the distinction between interaction and fusion. For too long, the church has abandoned ancient Christian disciplines due to fear. Many new-age thoughts are simply newly packaged old deception. *God in us* is an entirely different belief than *God is us*.

[21] Direct the participants toward the Psalms. Together, identify timeless prayers and then practice personalizing them. Scripture-praying will be absolutely revolutionary for many souls.

Chapter-by-Chapter Discussion Guide

[18] Faith as a Duet

Reading:
- In your daily life, do you believe that God is equally present in every moment?
- How can your answer affect your communion with God?
- What is the difference between making something first and making something center?

Thought Focus: What daily event did you select for this exercise? Share any discoveries you made.

Exercise: How did it feel to "tell God things He already knows" and "purpose to converse" with Him in the moment to moment of daily life?

[19] Our Primary Occupation

Reading:

- Of the three job descriptions Jesus gave to the disciples in Mark 3, which is most intuitive for your personality? Which is most applauded in your spiritual community?
- How might the disciples have felt as Jesus said, "I am with you always" as He ascended out of sight?
- What thoughts and reactions do you have to Alicia's closing statement that "the priority job description of a Jesus-follower is still literal."

Thought Focus: Share any reflections from reading John 11 as you considered the early disciples' experience of Jesus. What does it mean to you personally and practically that Jesus is with you always?

Exercise: Share any principles you gleaned from your interviews.

[20] Invited Home

Reading:

- Restate Alicia's assertion in your own words: ". . . making our home in Jesus—being with Him—is less about physical geography and more about spiritual gravity. Remaining in Jesus is less about external activity and more about interior attentiveness."

- When you pray, do you more often picture God as "out there, somewhere" or at home in your spirit?
- How might viewing each moment as an invitation to abide in Christ alter your everyday perspectives?

Thought Focus: Are there any spaces in your life in which the reality of "Christ in you" brings you comfort? Discomfort?

Exercise: Share your experiments with the listed practical suggestions or any other options you explored to practice the presence of God more fully.

[21] Inheritance Prayers

Reading:
- What do you most often pray for yourself?
- Consider Psalm 121. What could happen if an entire group scripture-prayed Psalm 121 over their lives daily for a month?
- Though all Scripture is (thankfully) for all people, share any scriptures that seem to consistently and deeply encourage you time after time. What eternal truths and principles from these scriptures can you pray over your life?

Thought Focus: How did it feel to ask God about His thoughts toward you? Refreshing? Silly? New?

Exercise: What did you experience as you wrote Scripture-prayers for yourself?

MOVEMENT/WEEK SIX:
RELATING TO HIS WORD

	READING SUMMARY	EXERCISE EMPHASIS
22	Has access to the Bible led to apathy about God's Word?	Study and relate to John 14–17.
23	Without grounding in the Word, we are like kites without strings	Study and relate to John 14–17.
24	The psalmist's relationship with the Word	Study and relate to John 14–17.
25	What God's voice can accomplish in a soul that listens and obeys	Study and relate to John 14–17.
26	Prayers to God for greater relationships with His Word	Study and relate to John 14–17.

Optional Supplementary Resources

How to Read the Bible for All Its Worth by Gordon D. Fee
and Douglas Stuart

*Eat This Book: A Conversation in the Art of Spiritual
Reading* by Eugene Peterson

"Why the Bible?" by Ravi Zacharias at the University of
Illinois on YouTube

"Is the Bible Reliable?" by NewChristian.org.uk

"Can You Trust the Bible?" by Josh McDowell at
PowerToChange.org

"Can I Trust the Bible?" by Glenn Harris at GospelOutreach.net

Optional Memory Verses

Your word is a lamp for my feet, a light on my path. (Psalm
119:105)

The decrees of the LORD are firm, and all of them are
   righteous. (Psalm 19:9b)
I have hidden your word in my heart that I might not sin
   against you. (Psalm 119:11)
Your decrees are the theme of my song wherever I lodge.
   (Psalm 119:54)
Your hands made me and formed me; give me understanding
   to learn your commands. (Psalm 119:73)

Chapter-by-Chapter Facilitator Notes

The five readings of this movement focus on recapturing a reverence
for the Word. I am deeply concerned about the lack of the Word
in our generation. God interrupted my atheistic existence through
an undeniable encounter. But He anchored my faith in His Word
through the mentoring of extraordinary Bible teachers. If we emphasize experience alone, we leave believers vulnerable to temptation and
deception, especially in dry, challenging, and disappointing seasons.

The exercises will be thrilling and revolutionary for some and
tedious and boring for others. That is okay. Speak of these exercises
as the development of a fundamental skill.

[22] Though it may seem unnerving as a facilitator not to have
definitive answers for any doubts participants express about
the Bible, guide participants in the discipline of holding
their questions in God's presence. Challenge them to live
the doubt *with* God. Honesty, held in God's presence, leads
to deeper intimacy with Him.

[23] This reading could touch a nerve in your group. It may help
to think of the Bible as the expert mentor in the pursuit of
intimacy with God. In any sincere endeavor, wisdom invites
us to learn from experts. In other areas (health, education,

work), what might motivate someone to dismiss the opportunity to consult a readily available expert?

[24] At first glance, Psalm 119 can appear repetitive. Help participants picture a human writing these words. What is the writer's subject? What emotions does the writer express toward his subject? What overlapping themes are present? Through such questions, we can help participants catch from the author what words alone cannot teach.

[25] Attempt to make the poetry of Psalm 119 practical by asking, "Do you think the author was always filled with joy or always without sin because he meditated on God's Word? What, then, was he expressing as he penned the psalm?"

[26] As this movement concludes, invite participants to share how their thoughts toward the Bible have shifted or changed. Lead them in responding to this prompt: "In one year, I would like my relationship with the Bible to be characterized by _____."

Chapter-by-Chapter Discussion Guide

[22] The Word

Reading:

- Imagine that you are John writing John 1:1–2 about Jesus. In your own words, what was John trying to communicate to his readers?
- Regarding honoring the Bible, has "access led to apathy" in your culture?
- "Somehow, King David's 'Your Word is a lamp to my feet' has deteriorated into 'Your Word is optional to my faith-walk.'" Do you agree or disagree with this statement from Alicia?

Thought Focus: What thoughts came to your mind in response to the question, "What do I really believe about God's Word?"

Exercise: Describe any discoveries or observations from your time of study.

[23] A Kite Without a String

Reading:
- In your own words, what did the young man on the plane believe about the Scriptures?
- What factors might contribute to how flippantly many dismiss the Word's weight in your culture?
- Consider the reality of a kite without a string. What is attractive? Destructive?

Thought Focus: Which line of Psalm 19:7–11 is most meaningful to you today?

Exercise: Did any patterns emerge in your study?

[24] To God About God's Word

Reading:
- The subject of the psalmist's poem is the Word: God's laws, precepts, statutes, commands, and decrees. What current cultural realities affect how rarely verbs like *delight*, *rejoice*, *love*, and *consumed* are connected to nouns like *laws*, *decrees*, and *commands*?
- In your own words, rephrase Psalm 119:120: "I stand in awe of your laws."
- Imagine being mentored by this psalmist. Picture yourself meeting weekly for coffee. What do you think would characterize his perspective on life?

Thought Focus: Think through how you would explain Psalm 119:11 to a child. How can hiding God's Word in your heart help you not to sin against Him?

Exercise: Were any sentences especially mysterious, intriguing, or puzzling to you?

[25] When the Word Is Heard and Heeded

Reading:
- What thought, image, or phrase stood out to you the most from Alicia's personal story?
- In a few sentences, describe your journey with the Word of God. For example, "As a child, the Bible was just the biggest book in the house. I bought a Bible in my twenties after hearing a minister speak from 1 Corinthians 13 at a wedding. Today, I try to read every day, but it often feels dry."
- Which, if any, of the listed daily prayers does God frequently hear from you? Write down the corresponding scripture and try to read it daily for a week.

Thought Focus: Share any scriptures that came to mind as you paused to pray.

Exercise: What do you think Jesus' words in John 15–16 might have meant to the original hearers?

[26] A Request for More

Reading:
- The psalmist was a literate, educated, gifted writer and leader. Guess how many people on the planet cannot read or write and how many people are without a Bible in their first

language. Visit UIS.UNESCO.org and Wycliffe.org to check
your guesses.

- How do you think this psalmist kept his passion for God's
  Word in the midst of his academic, intellectual, and spiritual
  privileges?
- Brainstorm ways you can nurture an ache for more of
  God's Word.

Thought Focus: Share any phrases or thoughts that stood out to you
from the three-thousand-year-old prayers.

Exercise: How do you think this five-chapter emphasis on Bible
study has impacted you? Are there any practices you would like to
incorporate into your life going forward?

MOVEMENT/WEEK SEVEN:
DISCOVERING GOD-PRINTS

	READING SUMMARY	EXERCISE EMPHASIS
27	Description of a sploshy soul	Identify how you connect with God.
28	A challenge for visionaries and volunteers	Take an action step to nurture your God-print.
29	A story of how we are all created to know Him	Draft a personal God-print statement.
30	The discipline of gratitude	Develop gratitude practices.
31	Lessons on the power of pure pleasure from Eric Liddell	Exercise the discipline of celebration.

Optional Supplementary Resources

Spiritual Disciplines Handbook by Adele Ahlberg Calhoun
The Wired Soul by Tricia McCary Rhodes

Optional Memory Verses

For you created my inmost being; you knit me together in
my mother's womb. (Psalm 139:13)

You created all things, and by your will they were created
and have their being. (Revelation 4:11)

Devote yourselves to prayer, being watchful and thankful.
(Colossians 4:2)

For the LORD takes delight in his people; he crowns the
humble with victory. Let his faithful people rejoice
in this honor and sing for joy on their beds. (Psalm
149:4–5)

Chapter-by-Chapter Facilitator Notes

This movement calls readers to consider the truth that they are personally saturated with God's fingerprints. God custom designed us
to know Him. You may be surprised who struggles with this movement. Some of the most faithful, hard-working servants have settled
in their minds long ago that intimacy with God is for others. Settle
in your heart your theology in this matter so that you can whole-
heartedly encourage them to discover their God-prints.

[27] This chapter invites participants to consider how God
uniquely crafted them to experience Him. Some may feel
uncomfortable personalizing God's love in this way and prefer to deflect to a one-size-fits-all experience of God. Calling
on parenting images can guide them away from viewing
such personalization as a form of narcissism toward recog-
nizing it as a means of honoring God's love and creativity.

[28] We often believe that the height of Christian maturity is
service. But ancient writers speak of love for God, others,

and ourselves as the true fruit of maturity. Some form of faith crisis often creates the bridge between service and love. Emphasize that the wall will become a door for those who live it, lean into it, and stay present to the disappointment that created it.

[29] Viewing ourselves as God's art exposes areas in which shame still shadows us. Place the topic on the table and discuss how shame's agenda is separation from God.

[30] Grandma Ella did not suddenly choose gratitude in her nineties. Neither will we. The choices we make today absolutely influence who we will become in the future. With your group, consider how the principle of sowing and reaping applies to the attitudes we nurture today and who we become.

[31] In this final chapter of movement seven, take time to ask participants how the movement has affected their understanding of practicing the presence of God. Encourage them to write down anything they never want to forget about God's personal love for them.

Chapter-by-Chapter Discussion Guide

[27] Sploshy

Reading:

- What is the difference between how Alicia defines *sploshy* and emotionalism?
- What do you notice about yourself when your spirit is saturated with God's presence? What changes do you notice in your attitudes, actions, or thoughts?
- Make a list of people who seem to leave a sploshy watermark wherever they go. What similarities do they share?

Thought Focus: How sploshy has your leadership been lately?

Exercise: Was it easy or difficult to identify contexts or experiences that water your love for God?

[28] A Wall and a Door

Reading:

- Have you ever hit a wall where your faith went cold in service or leadership? If so, what emotions and thoughts marked the experience?
- What is the difference between *passion* and *intimacy* with regard to our relationship with God?

Thought Focus: Does anything feel familiar to you in the spiritual profile of a passionate visionary or diligent church worker?

Exercise: How can we, as a group, encourage one another to prioritize practices that nourish our souls?

[29] Our Original Artist

Reading:

- Say the following aloud: "I am God's art. He created me. I exist by divine design." On any given day, how hard or easy is it to believe this statement?
- Have you ever had a physical weakness that has spiritually taught you to lean on God?
- Thinking of how God has crafted you to know Him, what activities might the two of you do together in heaven?

Thought Focus: As you personalized Esther Adanna's story, were any parts especially difficult or particularly moving?

Exercise: Share, if you feel comfortable, your God-print statement.

[30] An Internal Air Freshener

Reading:

- Alicia states, "Aging seems its own wilderness." Think of elderly saints whose company you enjoy. What qualities or characteristics do you admire?
- In your own words, describe the connection between gratitude as a discipline and practicing the presence of God.
- Pause to identify seven moments in the last twenty-four hours for which you can specifically and genuinely give thanks.

Thought Focus: What life choices can you discern in the journeys of saints whose spirits become sweeter with time?

Exercise: Share any gratitude practices—new or old—that you plan to incorporate into your life as a guardian of intimacy with God.

[31] The Positive Power of Pure Pleasure

Reading:

- Liddell did not edit his running style to make it more professional or presentable. Pause for a moment to recall any time you edited yourself to fit in. What drove that decision?
- Alicia asserts, "Excellence does not authenticate our God-prints." Do you agree or disagree with this statement? Why?
- Imagine Liddell in the prison camp. Picture the children, mothers, and fathers that he touched in Jesus' name. Why might hell have trembled at Liddell's imprisoned life?

Thought Focus: What activities or practices filled in the blank for you in this thought focus?

Exercise: Do you lean toward extroversion or introversion? What does celebration look like if you are being true to you?

MOVEMENT/WEEK EIGHT: THE DISCIPLINE OF RESTRAINT

	READING SUMMARY	EXERCISE EMPHASIS
32	*Can ≠ should*	Complete a simple meal fast.
33	The discipline of restraint in Jesus' life	Rest a strength.
34	The discipline of mental waiting	Fast rehash of the past and sin-hunts.
35	The discipline of earthly simplicity	Fast enough+.
36	The discipline of purity of soul	Evaluate how me time is spent.

Optional Supplementary Resources

Adrenaline and Stress: The Exciting New Breakthrough That Helps You Overcome Stress Damage by Archibald Hart
40 Days of Decrease: A Different Kind of Hunger. A Different Kind of Fast by Alicia Britt Chole

Optional Memory Verses

[Jesus declared,] "For I have come down from heaven not to do my will but to do the will of him who sent me." (John 6:38)

I love the Father and do exactly what my Father has commanded me. (John 14:31)

You will keep in perfect peace those whose minds are steadfast, because they trust in you. (Isaiah 26:3)

For where your treasure is, there your heart will be also. (Matthew 6:21)

"I have the right to do anything," you say—but not everything is beneficial. "I have the right to do anything"—but not everything is constructive. (1 Corinthians 10:23)

Chapter-by-Chapter Facilitator Notes

This may be among the more unfamiliar themes of *The Sacred Slow*. We often think that God gave us strengths to use *always*. As the group considers the different forms of restraint, some may ask for formulas because they do not want to "miss God." Encourage them to exercise the disciplines of stillness and listening that they have been developing. The Holy Spirit promises to lead us personally into all truth. His guidance is our common pursuit.

[32] The discipline of restraint requires discernment. Be prepared to open up the discussion to how imperfect humans can ever assume they know anything about the will of a perfect God.

[33] The Scriptures do not record every minute of Jesus' public ministry (John 21:25). Consider how many sick individuals must have been in need of healing in Jesus' day. Yet He walked by entire towns without pausing. Consider how many desired to hear Him speak. Yet He did not always stay where crowds were gathering. Opportunity is not the only indicator of God's will. To help wrap examples around this concept, think of times in which God has called you to restrain. Come prepared to share from your experience.

[34] Frame this application in terms of months and years, instead of days and weeks. Growing a disciplined mind in an undisciplined age is extremely difficult. Pose questions to the group such as, "What expectations would be reasonable? Unreasonable? Miraculous?" Remind the group that staying in the struggle *is* the victory.

[35] If love for God is not what motivates the disciplines of simplifying and giving, the actions have minimal—if not negative—impact on our spiritual formation. Only love can turn disciplines into worship. Ask what other motivations can inspire simplifying and giving. Contrast the fruit of

those motivations with the fruit of being motivated by the love of God.

[36] Some participants may hunger for lists to make obedience easier. Without listening, lists lead to legalism. Challenge the group to press into moment-by-moment listening and dependence.

Chapter-by-Chapter Discussion Guide

[32] Can ≠ Should

Reading:

- Discerning when *can ≠ should* requires slower disciplines such as listening, waiting, and stillness. Why are slower disciplines perceived as harder disciplines in our day?
- In your own words, what is the difference (externally and internally) between timidity, passivity, and restraint?
- Share a time when someone wanted you to "push ahead" but you chose to "live led."

Thought Focus: Share any insights from John 7:2–6.

Exercise: Was the concept of a Bridegroom Fast new or familiar? What was the hardest part of the fast?

[33] Living *Led*

Reading:

- Alicia states, "Jesus' led was muscular and authoritative." Where else in the Gospels do you see evidence of the discipline of restraint in Jesus' life?
- Internally, how do you know if you are submitting a strength to God and His timing?

- How vulnerable do you feel to the woo of scenery, crowds, and opportunity?

Thought Focus: How do you know when you are inspired by opportunity or inspired by God?

Exercise: How did it feel to rest a strength?

[34] Mental Waiting

Reading:
- What does Alicia mean by "mental waiting"?
- Is controlling your thought flow a new or familiar concept to you?
- What are some of the greatest challenges you face in "taming and training" your mind?

Thought Focus: Did you experience any frustration in responding to this thought focus?

Exercise: Which of the two suggested fasts proved easier for you?

[35] Earthly Simplicity

Reading:
- Have you ever witnessed a natural disaster or seen its aftermath? What do survivors most often identify as the greatest loss in such tragedies?
- Pause for a few moments to think of the people around you. Silently ask God how you can remind them of their preciousness to you and to Him.
- "Lives are worth dying for. So perhaps they should receive more of our investment." Share one way in which you can tangibly invest value in your relationships today.

Thought Focus: What thoughts did you have during this invitation to simplify and give?

Exercise: Did you notice any internal resistance in this exercise?

[36] Purity of Soul

Reading:
- Recall the three tests of true biblical freedom.
- How can lawlessness masquerade as liberty?
- What signs might indicate that we are *using* our bodies instead of *stewarding* our bodies?

Thought Focus: How do you personally distinguish between legalism and voluntary restraint?

Exercise: Did you struggle in any way during this exercise? If so, describe the struggle and its source.

MOVEMENT/WEEK NINE: A THEOLOGY OF TIME AND SPACE

	READING SUMMARY	EXERCISE EMPHASIS
37	Is time a gift or a grinch?	Take a poll of our attitudes toward time.
38	A consideration of the patterns of time	Chart a year's intensity.
39	Our need for margin	Conduct an interview.
40	Space-shaping saboteurs	Take steps to steward time.

Optional Supplementary Resources

Margin: Restoring Emotional, Physical, Financial, and Time Reserves to Overloaded Lives by Richard Swenson
Ordering Your Private World by Gordon MacDonald

Optional Memory Verses

Teach us to number our days, that we may gain a heart of wisdom. (Psalm 90:12)

There is a time for everything, and a season for every activity under the heavens. (Ecclesiastes 3:1)

Chapter-by-Chapter Facilitator Notes

Personally, I consider this to be one of the more fun movements. I delight to see participants discover rhythms in their lives and shape their space accordingly.

[37] Most of us inherit our starting view of time either from models we unconsciously adopted or models we consciously rejected. Be prepared to help participants respond with grace to those who influenced their perspectives on time. Such influencers were also influenced by others and by the reality of life in a very different age.

[38] Scheduling is not necessarily synonymous with shaping. The former is about making order, and the latter is about taking authority. Encourage the participants not to confuse being orderly with being disciplined. Time is a gift to be stewarded.

[39] We all have different energy levels. It can be challenging for those with high energy not to dismiss those with low energy

as "uncommitted." Start a discussion with your group about the factors that can affect a person's energy level. Ask, "Whatever a person's starting energy level, what could be the short-term and long-term consequences of overextending into the red zone?"

[40] Guide your group in generating a list of possible motivations for saying yes. Then identify which ones could be sustainable. Ask the group to describe how they feel when others are disappointed with or in them. Open the floor for them to share if anyone has ever used that feeling to manipulate or control them. Brainstorm how to practically resist and release the fear of disappointing others.

Chapter-by-Chapter Discussion Guide

[37] Gift or Grinch?

Reading:

- How *did* you feel about time when you woke up this morning?
- Alicia paints a picture of God lovingly waiting for you to awaken. How natural does that image feel to you?
- What might change in the life of a soul who stopped viewing time as "a captive of chaos" and started viewing time as "a servant of sovereignty"?

Thought Focus: What one sentence describes your working definition of time?

Exercise: How did you feel when the poll results came rolling in?

[38] The Flow of Time

Reading:

- What do you think Alicia means by "shaping the space of our lives"?
- Are there any months or seasons in which you are often blue? Happy? Under the weather? Stressed? Relationally supported?
- How would mislabeling patterns as unexpected surprises affect someone psychologically?

Thought Focus: Does your energy distribution reflect your values?

Exercise: Which months are typically more responsibility-intense for you? Do you have time beforehand to store up energy or afterward to refuel?

[39] Margin

Reading:

- What was it about the dishes that might have been the "last straw" for Alicia's weary soul?
- How can you know when going the extra mile for a worthy cause is crossing over into debilitating burnout?
- Have you ever lived in the red zone of burnout? If you feel comfortable, describe how it felt emotionally, spiritually, mentally, and relationally.

Thought Focus: When was the last time you said one of the four opening sentences to yourself?

Exercise: Share any insights from the interview you conducted.

[40] Space-Shaping Saboteurs

Reading:

- For your wiring, which extreme is more stressful: taking life as it comes or scheduling out every hour? Describe a schedule that would truly serve you.
- If Superman Time Syndrome felt familiar, feel free to tell a story of yourself to illustrate the point.

Think about your responsibilities tomorrow. What would the nth degree look like for you? Thought Focus: What kind of requests are the hardest for you to decline?

Exercise: What would need to change for your schedule to reflect your values?

MOVEMENT/WEEK TEN: UNEXPECTED FRIENDS

	READING SUMMARY	EXERCISE EMPHASIS
41	The cost of Jesus' "Follow Me"	Interview those who inspire you to love God.
42	The mystery of suffering	Respond to quotes on suffering.
43	The gift of God's silence	Interview the wise on when they speak and when they are silent.
44	A friend called failure	Consider your responses to failure.

Optional Supplementary Resources

The Cost of Discipleship by Dietrich Bonhoeffer

The Screwtape Letters by C. S. Lewis

Optional Memory Verses

"Come, follow me," Jesus said. (Matthew 4:19)

Now I rejoice in what I am suffering for you, and I fill up in my flesh what is still lacking in regard to Christ's afflictions, for the sake of his body, which is the church. (Colossians 1:24)

I waited patiently for the LORD; he turned to me and heard my cry. (Psalm 40:1)

[Jesus said to Peter,] "And when you have turned back, strengthen your brothers." (Luke 22:32b)

Chapter-by-Chapter Facilitator Notes

Though painful, participants will emerge from this movement with hope that their suffering is not in vain. Be prepared to listen a lot and pray. Your gift to participants in this movement is providing a safe place for honest processing.

[41] *Free will. God's sovereignty. The existence of evil.* Get ready for more questions about the existence of pain in the world! Spend time thinking through your own angst about these concepts. Resist the urge to tidy up your responses, and offer, "I struggle with that too" where appropriate. Honesty is a friend of intimacy with God.

[42] Review John 11 in preparation for this movement. Consider Mary's and Martha's responses to Jesus and His response to them. "If you had been here . . ." is a means of asking, "Where *were* you?" Remind the group that *then* and *now*, Jesus responds to sincere questions with mercy.

[43] On paper or a whiteboard, write *God's silence* in the middle of the space with lines extending from the center like an idea

web. Brainstorm what assumptions we make about God's silence. Then erase or cross out any assumptions that are inconsistent with His character. Evaluating assumptions is a powerful investment in soul health.

[44] Compare and contrast the desire to avoid failure with the desire to avoid sin. The two are not always synonymous. What signs can indicate that we are more concerned about others seeing our failure than actually sinning against God?

Chapter-by-Chapter Discussion Guide

[41] Where Follow Leads

Reading:

- In the beginning of your faith journey, where did you think that Jesus' "Follow Me" would lead you?
- What parts of Jesus' story would you rather skip in your own journey?
- Many ask why God allowed the Fall in the first place, since it opened the door to such pain in the world. Brainstorm alternatives. In other words, what would be necessary in order for disobedience to be impossible for humans?

Thought Focus: What unexpected places have startled you in your spiritual journey?

Exercise: Did any common threads emerge from your interviews?

[42] An Ancient Angst

Reading:

- How are questions about pain and questions about God's character related?

- Attempt to restate Hebrews 5:7–10 in your own words.
- From your experience with suffering, can you personally affirm any of the outcomes of suffering identified in Hebrews 5:7–10?

Thought Focus: Share any perspective shifts you experienced during this thought focus.

Exercise: Read Lewis's quote again. Why is obedience in the midst of dark times a powerful spiritual weapon?

[43] The Silence of God

Reading:
- Do you tend to associate God's silence with God's love, discipline, absence, or disappointment?
- Think of one area in your life that you desperately wish were different. Form that ache into a specific prayer to God.
- God's ways are infinitely higher than ours, but what might inspire God to offer silence instead of explanations to us?

Thought Focus: Share your responses to the quote from John of the Cross.

Exercise: Share a time when a friend's silent presence was more healing than any words he or she could have offered.

[44] A Friend Called Failure

Reading:
- What unintended consequences can result when a parent—often inspired by their definition of love—rescues their child from experiencing failure?
- How can failure be a friend of spiritual formation?

- Quietly reflect on sin-inspired failures in your life. Take a moment to thank God for the situations that exposed sin in your soul.

Thought Focus: Though it does not change the past, how can reframing mistakes as teachers affect your future?

Exercise: Share any reflections you had on Peter's failure and restoration.

MOVEMENT/WEEK ELEVEN: SABBATH AND PRAYER RETREATS

	READING SUMMARY	EXERCISE EMPHASIS
45	Identifying Sabbath space in real life	Assess the space for rest in your life.
46	Taking a prayer retreat, part one	Research possibilities for prayer retreating.
47	Taking a prayer retreat, part two	Take a one-to-three-hour mini-retreat.
48	Taking a prayer retreat, part three	Learn how to evaluate your retreat.

Optional Supplementary Resources

The Rest of God: Restoring Your Soul by Restoring Sabbath by Mark Buchanan

The Sabbath by Abraham Joshua Heschel

Mudhouse Sabbath: An Invitation to a Life of Spiritual Discipline by Lauren F. Winner

Optional Memory Verses

Remember the Sabbath day by keeping it holy. (Exodus 20:8)

Come with me by yourselves to a quiet place and get some
rest. (Mark 6:31)

This is what the Sovereign LORD, the Holy One of Israel,
says: "In repentance and rest is your salvation, in
quietness and trust is your strength." (Isaiah 30:15)

Chapter-by-Chapter Facilitator Notes

This movement addresses the reality that it takes work to experience
sabbath rest and then introduces the discipline of prayer retreating.
I focus on retreating because there seems to be less literature on the
subject.

Encourage participants to pursue a retreat regardless of its length.
Some may have glorious first retreats. Others may come back frustrated that the time felt flat. Remind them again and again that
retreating is about love (not emotion) and discipline (not productivity).
Like working out, a steady practice of retreating builds spiritual muscle
that powerfully enhances daily intimacy with God.

[45] Be prepared to facilitate a discussion on whether the Sabbath
commandment today means any day a week, Friday sunset
to Saturday sunset, Sundays . . . or something else entirely.
Consider what "keeping [the Sabbath] holy" might mean
to God.

[46] A question may arise regarding whether prayer retreating
is a function of personality. One of the myths that needs
debunking is that the only way to have a still spirit is to
have a still body. Some retreat as they walk, hike, garden, or
paint. Encourage participants to reconsider their God-print
statements and do what helps them focus on God.

[47] Invest time in helping the group recall the work God did
in them during the God-concepts movement. How we view

God drastically impacts how we think He wants us to spend a retreat and even *if* we think He wants us to take a retreat. Though twenty-four hours is a worthy goal, urge everyone to start somewhere, however small it may seem.

[48] Especially if several in your group cannot take a full day for retreating, discuss ways in which the participants can help one another make space for mini-retreats. Plan a debrief session after the retreat experiences to help normalize frustrations and inspire further experiments.

Chapter-by-Chapter Discussion Guide

[45] The Work of Rest

Reading:

- When you were growing up, what did *Sabbath* mean in your home?
- Share any ways in which the Sabbath is different from any other day of the week for you now.
- Dream. In one year, what would you like the Sabbath to look like for you?

Thought Focus: Share Sabbath practices you have seen or practiced that helped keep the day holy.

Exercise: How much white space for sabbath rest is currently in your life? Identify one small step you can take toward keeping Sabbath.

[46] Come Away

Reading:

- Share your honest responses to the suggestion of devoting one day a month to prayer retreating.

- As a group, do a cost analysis of a prayer retreat to weigh the expenses and benefits of the investment.
- How do you feel when someone simply enjoys your company without wanting anything? How might God feel when we offer Him the gift of time with no strings attached?

Thought Focus: What objections came to your mind with regard to prayer retreating?

Exercise: Share any research findings that surprised or encouraged you.

[47] Packing Light

Reading:
- Whom do you need to consider when setting a date for a retreat?
- Which option for a space (monastery, hotel, friend's home, nature center, other) seemed most inviting to you?
- Did you experience any pangs of panic or worries about withdrawal at the thought of leaving certain things at home? If so, form that concern into a prayer and let it rest in God's presence.

Thought Focus: What did your ten- to sixty-minute mini-retreat look like?

Exercise: Share any insights, frustrations, victories, and disappointments from your one- to three-hour mini-retreat.

[48] Retreat Rhythms

Reading:
- Brainstorm ways to practically focus on God's character for your retreat.

- Alicia speaks of how worship-led repentance is "clean." How is this different from repentance motivated by worry or witch hunts?
- What is your honest response to the thought of taking a nap—even a long one—on your retreat? What might God think of this use of time?

Thought Focus: Share any reflections from your meditation on Isaiah 30.

Exercise: "Let God measure the fruit." What is your guess regarding how you and God might measure fruit differently?

MOVEMENT/WEEK TWELVE: THE SACRED GO

	READING SUMMARY	EXERCISE EMPHASIS
49	The overflow of *The Sacred Slow*	Evaluate your Personal Inventory.
50	Living with open eyes	Cultivate awareness as a witness.
51	Why Alicia wrote *The Sacred Slow*	Make a plan to invest in others.
52	Anticipating the fruit of the next season	Add to your Life Scroll.

Optional Supplementary Resources

In the Name of Jesus by Henri J. M. Nouwen
The Master Plan of Evangelism by Robert Coleman

Optional Memory Verses

And let us run with perseverance the race marked out for us. (Hebrews 12:1b)

I tell you, open your eyes and look at the fields! They are
ripe for harvest. (John 4:35)

And the things you have heard me say in the presence of
many witnesses entrust to reliable people who will also
be qualified to teach others. (2 Timothy 2:2)

Stand at the crossroads and look; ask for the ancient paths,
ask where the good way is, and walk in it, and you will
find rest for your souls. (Jeremiah 6:16)

Chapter-by-Chapter Facilitator Notes

[49] Ending well is perhaps more important than starting well.
Often we trample endings with new beginnings. Endings
need resting space. Encourage participants to remain fully
present for this last week of *The Sacred Slow*. As a group,
discuss how to savor this ending without sabotaging the next
beginning.

[50] One size does not fit all with regards to witness. Initiate a
discussion on what can inspire seekers to follow Christians
to Jesus. Authenticity is today's currency. Affirm the various
ways that intimacy with the same God manifests in different
ways in different lives.

[51] The choice to focus interpersonally in this final movement
is quite intentional. Keep emphasizing the concept of overflow to link personal soul health with interpersonal love and
fruitful service.

[52] This last note is personally for you as a facilitator. Thank
you for partnering with me in awakening our generation
to sustainable nearness with God! Thank you for faithfully
leading your tribe through this departure from Fast Faith!
My prayer is that you, too, have been strengthened as you
strengthened others. Be sure to rest, celebrate, and bask in

the Father's "well done, good and faithful servant." And if you have time, send me a note about your experience. I would love to learn from you.

Chapter-by-Chapter Discussion Guide

[49] The Overflow

Reading:

- Alicia speaks of an ancient error that equates "visible increase with God's favor and visible decrease with man's failure." How vulnerable do you feel to this error?
- Reread the description of Jesus' life as overflow. What changes would you like to see in your life in the coming years?
- Picture God placing a crown of forgiveness and love on your head. Then pray for friends whose heads are weighed down by shame to meet your gracious and generous Savior.

Thought Focus: What comments (if any) have those near you made about you during *The Sacred Slow* journey?

Exercise: Share any mental shifts you experienced as you evaluated your Personal Inventory in terms of movement instead of accomplishment.

[50] Open Eyes

Reading:

- What might the townspeople have thought or felt as they interacted with the Twelve?
- What were the twelve leaders missing that one sinner found? In other words, why did the Samaritan woman's moments

with Jesus inspire a citywide revival when the disciples' 24/7
with Jesus did not?

- By nature and nurture, do you tend to view witness as the
  focus of seasonal events or as the daily overflow of gratitude
  and love?

Thought Focus: What did you see today in response to your prayer
for "open eyes"?

Exercise: Was it easier to truly "see" certain people more than
others? If so, did you notice any patterns? For example, is it more
natural for you to truly see people when you are working or
relaxing? When they are older or younger? When they look like you
or look different from you?

[51] You+

Reading:

- Be honest: Did you think you would really make it to
  chapter 51?
- Brainstorm ways to intentionally pass on what you have
  learned from the Sacred Slow experience.
- "Life is not the offspring of paper or programs." In your own
  words, what is Alicia trying to communicate through this
  statement?

Thought Focus: Identify some Timothys in whom you can invest
the principles of practicing the presence of God.

Exercise: What one thing from your Sacred Slow journey would
you like to see multiplied in the lives of those you love?

[52] Anticipation

Reading:

- What is the difference between *closure* and *transition*?
- How do you think God desires to be loved?
- Share two or three principles from *The Sacred Slow* that you never want to forget.

Thought Focus: What do you hope your life-as-a-movie sequel will feature?

Exercise: What dreams do you have for future additions to your Life Scroll?

MY PERSONAL INVENTORY

CHAPTER 7—LISTEN HEAVEN-DOWN.

My prayer: *What is Your heart for me in this season? What is Your focus as my Master Mentor? What emphasis would please You?*

My impressions:

_____

_____

_____

_____

Rough draft of this season's theme:

_____

_____

CHAPTER 8—PRAYERFULLY IDENTIFY AREA APPLICATIONS.

My prayer: *God, how would You like me to apply this heaven-down theme in my daily life physically? Relationally? With work? At home?*

My impressions:

_____

_____

_____

_____

Rough draft of areas of application:

AREA	APPLICATION

CHAPTER 9—INVITE TRUSTED VOICES INTO THE PROCESS.

My questions: "What are your overall impressions as you read my Personal Inventory? In your own words, what is the broad theme that God is speaking over my life? Do any of the specific applications in any area appear unclear or unrealistic? Is there anything I have expressed concern over that is not represented in my inventory?"

Their feedback:

_____

_____

_____

_____

My revised season theme:

_____

_____

CHAPTER 49—EVALUATE HEAVEN-DOWN.

My prayer: *God, from Your perspective, was there* movement?

My impressions:

_____

_____

_____

_____

When I plan to listen heaven-down for my next season:

_____

JOHN 14–17

"Do not let your hearts be troubled. You believe in God;
believe also in me. My Father's house has many rooms; if
that were not so, would I have told you that I am going there
to prepare a place for you? And if I go and prepare a place for
you, I will come back and take you to be with me that you
also may be where I am. You know the way to the place
where I am going." Thomas said to him, "Lord, we don't
know where you are going, so how can we know the way?"
Jesus answered, "I am the way and the truth and the life. No
one comes to the Father except through me. If you really
know me, you will know my Father as well. From now on,
you do know him and have seen him." Philip said, "Lord,
show us the Father and that will be enough for us." Jesus
answered: "Don't you know me, Philip, even after I have
been among you such a long time? Anyone who has seen me
has seen the Father. How can you say, 'Show us the Father'?
Don't you believe that I am in the Father, and that the
Father is in me? The words I say to you I do not speak on my
own authority. Rather, it is the Father, living in me, who is
doing his work. Believe me when I say that I am in the
Father and the Father is in me; or at least believe on the
evidence of the works themselves. Very truly I tell you, whoever believes in me will do the works I have been doing, and
they will do even greater things than these, because I am
going to the Father. And I will do whatever you ask in my

name, so that the Father may be glorified in the Son. You may ask me for anything in my name, and I will do it. If you love me, keep my commands. And I will ask the Father, and he will give you another advocate to help you and be with you forever—the Spirit of truth. The world cannot accept him, because it neither sees him nor knows him. But you know him, for he lives with you and will be in you. I will not leave you as orphans; I will come to you. Before long, the world will not see me anymore, but you will see me. Because I live, you also will live. On that day you will realize that I am in my Father, and you are in me, and I am in you. Whoever has my commands and keeps them is the one who loves me. The one who loves me will be loved by my Father, and I too will love them and show myself to them." Then Judas (not Judas Iscariot) said, "But, Lord, why do you intend to show yourself to us and not to the world?" Jesus replied, "Anyone who loves me will obey my teaching. My Father will love them, and we will come to them and make our home with them. Anyone who does not love me will not obey my teaching. These words you hear are not my own; they belong to the Father who sent me. All this I have spoken while still with you. But the Advocate, the Holy Spirit, whom the Father will send in my name, will teach you all things and will remind you of everything I have said to you. Peace I leave with you; my peace I give you. I do not give to you as the world gives. Do not let your hearts be troubled and do not be afraid. You heard me say, 'I am going away and I am coming back to you.' If you loved me, you would be glad that I am going to the Father, for the Father is greater than I. I have told you now before it happens, so that when it does happen you will believe. I will not say much more to you, for the prince of this world is coming. He has no hold over me, but he comes so that the world may learn that I love the Father and do exactly what my Father has commanded me. Come now; let us leave. I am the true vine, and my Father is the gardener. He cuts off every branch in me that bears no fruit, while every branch that does bear fruit he prunes so that it will be even more fruitful. You are already clean because of the word I have spoken to you. Remain in me, as I also remain in you. No branch can bear fruit by itself; it must remain in the vine. Neither can you bear fruit unless you remain in me. I am the vine; you are the branches. If you remain in me and I in you, you will bear much fruit; apart from me you can do nothing. If you do not remain in me, you are like a branch that is thrown away and withers; such branches are picked up, thrown into the fire and burned. If you remain in me and my words remain in you, ask whatever you wish, and it will be done for you. This is to my Father's glory, that you bear much fruit, showing yourselves to be my disciples. As the Father has loved me, so have I loved you. Now remain in my love. If you keep my commands, you will remain in my love, just as I have kept my Father's commands and remain in his love. I have told you this so that my joy may be in you and that your joy may be complete. My command is this: Love each other as I have loved you. Greater love has no one than this: to lay down one's life for one's friends. You are my friends if you do what I command. I no longer call you servants, because a servant does not know his master's business. Instead, I have called you friends, for everything that I learned from my Father I have made known to you. You did not choose me, but I chose you and appointed you so that you might go and bear fruit—fruit that will last—and so that whatever you ask in my name the Father will give you. This is my command:

Love each other. If the world hates you, keep in mind that it hated me first. If you belonged to the world, it would love you as its own. As it is, you do not belong to the world, but I have chosen you out of the world. That is why the world hates you. Remember what I told you: 'A servant is not greater than his master.' If they persecuted me, they will persecute you also. If they obeyed my teaching, they will obey yours also. They will treat you this way because of my name, for they do not know the one who sent me. If I had not come and spoken to them, they would not be guilty of sin; but now they have no excuse for their sin. Whoever hates me hates my Father as well. If I had not done among them the works no one else did, they would not be guilty of sin. As it is, they have seen, and yet they have hated both me and my Father. But this is to fulfill what is written in their Law: 'They hated me without reason.' When the Advocate comes, whom I will send to you from the Father—the Spirit of truth who goes out from the Father—he will testify about me. And you also must testify, for you have been with me from the beginning. All this I have told you so that you will not fall away. They will put you out of the synagogue; in fact, the time is coming when anyone who kills you will think they are offering a service to God. They will do such things because they have not known the Father or me. I have told you this, so that when their time comes you will remember that I warned you about them. I did not tell you this from the beginning because I was with you, but now I am going to him who sent me. None of you asks me, 'Where are you going?' Rather, you are filled with grief because I have said these things. But very truly I tell you, it is for your good that I am going away. Unless I go away, the Advocate will not come to you; but if I go, I will send him to you. When he comes, he will prove the world to be in the wrong about sin and righteousness and judgment: about sin, because people do not believe in me; about righteousness, because I am going to the Father, where you can see me no longer; and about judgment, because the prince of this world now stands condemned. I have much more to say to you, more than you can now bear. But when he, the Spirit of truth, comes, he will guide you into all the truth. He will not speak on his own; he will speak only what he hears, and he will tell you what is yet to come. He will glorify me because it is from me that he will receive what he will make known to you. All that belongs to the Father is mine. That is why I said the Spirit will receive from me what he will make known to you." Jesus went on to say, "In a little while you will see me no more, and then after a little while you will see me." At this, some of his disciples said to one another, "What does he mean by saying, 'In a little while you will see me no more, and then after a little while you will see me,' and 'Because I am going to the Father'?" They kept asking, "What does he mean by 'a little while'? We don't understand what he is saying." Jesus saw that they wanted to ask him about this, so he said to them, "Are you asking one another what I meant when I said, 'In a little while you will see me no more, and then after a little while you will see me'? Very truly I tell you, you will weep and mourn while the world rejoices. You will grieve, but your grief will turn to joy. A woman giving birth to a child has pain because her time has come; but when her baby is born she forgets the anguish because of her joy that a child is born into the world. So with you: Now is your time of grief, but I will see you again and you will rejoice, and no one will take away your joy. In that day you will no longer ask me anything. Very truly I tell you, my Father will give you whatever you ask in my name. Until now you have not asked for anything in my name. Ask and you will receive, and your joy will be complete. Though I have been speaking figuratively, a time is coming when I will no longer use this kind of language but will tell you plainly about my Father. In that day you will ask in my name. I am not saying that I will ask the Father on your behalf. No, the Father himself loves you because you have loved me and have believed that I came from God. I came from the Father and entered the world; now I am leaving the world and going back to the Father." Then Jesus' disciples said, "Now you are speaking clearly and without figures of speech. Now we can see that you know all things and that you do not even need to have anyone ask you questions. This makes us believe that you came from God." "Do you now believe?" Jesus replied. "A time is coming and in fact has come when you will be scattered, each to your own home. You will leave me all alone. Yet I am not alone, for my Father is with me. I have told you these things, so that in me you may have peace. In this world you will have trouble. But take heart! I have overcome the world." After Jesus said this, he looked toward heaven and prayed: "Father, the hour has come. Glorify your Son, that your Son may glorify you. For you granted him authority over all people that he might give eternal life to all those you have given him. Now this is eternal life: that they know you, the only true God, and Jesus Christ, whom you have sent. I have brought you glory on earth by finishing the work you gave me to do. And now, Father, glorify me in your presence with the glory I had with you before the world began. I have revealed you to those whom you gave me out of the world. They were yours; you gave them to me and they have obeyed your word. Now they know that everything you have given me comes from you. For I gave them the words you gave me and they accepted them. They knew with certainty that I came from you, and they believed that you sent me. I pray for them. I am not praying for the world, but for those you have given me, for they are yours. All I have is yours, and all you have is mine. And glory has come to me through them. I will remain in the world no longer, but they are still in the world, and I am coming to you. Holy Father, protect them by the power of your name, the name you gave me, so that they may be one as we are one. While I was with them, I protected them and kept them safe by that name you gave me. None has been lost except the one doomed to destruction so that Scripture would be fulfilled. I am coming to you now, but I say these things while I am still in the world, so that they may have the full measure of my joy within them. I have given them your word and the world has hated them, for they are not of the world any more than I am of the world. My prayer is not that you take them out of the world but that you protect them from the evil one. They are not of the world, even as I am not of it. Sanctify them by the truth; your word is truth. As you sent me into the world, I have sent them into the world. For them I sanctify myself, that they too may be truly sanctified. My prayer is not for them alone. I pray also for those who will believe in me through their message, that all of them may be one, Father, just as you are in me and I am in you. May they also be in us so that the world may believe that you have sent me. I have given them the glory that you gave me, that they may be one as we are one—I in them and you in me—so that they may be brought to complete unity. Then the world will know that you sent me and have loved them even as you have loved me. Father, I want those you have given me to be with me where

I am, and to see my glory, the glory you have given me because you loved me before the creation of the world. Righteous Father, though the world does not know you, I know you, and they know that you have sent me. I have made you known to them, and will continue to make you known in order that the love you have for me may be in them and that I myself may be in them."

GOD-PRINT

God has created me in such a way that I thrive when

_____

_____

are present and

_____

_____

are absent. My spirit soaks up His presence through

_____

_____

and

_____

_____

Activities that drain that reserve are

_____

_____

and

_____

_____

So, a dream day for my spirit would be

_____

NOTES

Introduction
1. Alicia Britt Chole, *40 Days of Decrease: A Different Kind of Hunger. A Different Kind of Fast* (Nashville: W Publishing Group, 2015), 127.

Movement One
1. Michael Harter, ed., *Hearts on Fire: Praying with Jesuits* (Chestnut Hill, MA: Institute of Jesuit Sources, 2016), 102–3.

Chapter 2: What Is the Sacred Slow?
1. Brother Lawrence, *The Practice of the Presence of God* (Springdale, PA: Whitaker House, 1982), 81.

Chapter 3: The Number of Rest
1. Seven-day test (1 Samuel 13:8), seven demons (Mark 16:9; Luke 8:2), seven baskets (Matthew 15:37; Mark 8:8), seven years times two (Genesis 29:18, 27), seven sons (Acts 19:14), seven leaders (Acts 6:3), seven dips (2 Kings 5:10), seven rich years (Genesis 41:25–27), seven phrases (Matthew 26:46; Luke 23:34, 43, 46; John 19:26–27, 28, 30), seven searches (1 Kings 18:44), seven days of creation (Genesis 2:2–3), seven churches (Revelation 2–3), seven days marching (Joshua 6:15), seven times hotter (Daniel 3:19).

Chapter 4: The Original Sacred Slow
1. Endnotes make me happy. They provide space for an author to be guiltlessly geeky about research notes while still giving each reader the choice to read or skip them. But if you want more than I've included, you can read my academic essay "The Seventh Year" and access the corresponding bibliography at www.aliciabrittchole.com.

2. Turnham explains that the male slave "enters service as a result of poverty. . . . He has become one of the poor of the land, a status which not only humiliates the individuals, but also reprimands the other Hebrews. The concern of the entire Hebrew society is to remove this man from the status of being poor. . . . The Sabbath Year laws help the slave to escape the societal role of being poor." See Timothy John Turnham, "Male and Female Slaves in the Sabbath Year Laws of Exodus 21:1–11," *Society of Biblical Literature Seminar Papers* 26 (January 1, 1987): 548.

3. Moses' preparatory encouragement in Deuteronomy 15:12–15 implies that this release was to be accompanied by generous gifts of livestock, grain, and wine.

4. Discussion exists as to whether Hebrew indentured servants were to be freed in the seventh year of their service or during the community's Sabbath Year. See Robert Grady North's, "Maccabean Sabbath Years," *Biblica* 34, no. 4 (January 1, 1953): 503. However, since Deuteronomy discusses the freeing of indentured servants alongside the canceling of debts—a clarion emphasis of the seventh year (Deuteronomy 31:10)—I will include the release of indentured servants as a seventh-year component.

5. This prescribed Sabbath rest for the land included the following instructions: (1) the counting of years commenced upon entrance to the promised land; (2) the land could not be sown, pruned, or harvested for profit; (3) the regulation applied to farmland as well as vineyards and olive groves; and (4) whatever grew voluntarily in the land could be eaten by landowners, servants, hired workers, the poor, the alien, livestock, and wild animals.

6. On debt and usury in Israelite society, see Martin Goodman, "The First Jewish Revolt: Social Conflict and the Problem of Debt," *Journal of Jewish Studies* 33, no. 1–2 (March 1, 1982): 417–27.

7. In the seventh year, debts owed by fellow Israelites were to be cancelled as commanded in Deuteronomy 15:1–2: "This is how it is to be done: Every creditor shall cancel the loan they have made to a fellow Israelite. They shall not require payment from anyone among

their own people, because the Lord's time for canceling debts has been proclaimed." The language used in subsequent verses 3–18 emphasizes responsibility to the brotherhood, generosity toward the poor, the promised land as an inheritance, and a blessing that the obedient would become lenders instead of borrowers.

8. Every seventh year, during the Feast of Tabernacles, which ushered in the new year, all who resided in the promised land were to hear the law read as a community so that they could listen, learn, fear, and follow (Deuteronomy 31:9–13). The audience for this reading was inclusive regardless of age, gender, or even nationality. Resident aliens as well as children were to be assembled, because this command was a critical means of instructing the next generation in God's ways.

9. *The Jewish Encyclopedia* cites three possible reasons: (1) continuity with the creation-story seventh day, (2) ecological conservation and economic redistribution, and (3) the establishment of a God-ruled state "to promote the idea of theocracy: that one year in seven might be devoted 'to the Lord.'" See Isidore Singer, ed., *The Jewish Encyclopedia* (New York: Funk and Wagnals, 1906); s.v. "Sabbatical Year and Jubilee," accessed November 5, 2012, http://www. jewishencyclopedia.com/articles/12967-sabbatical-year-and-jubilee.

10. At the time of this writing, Dr. Shead was the head of the department of Old Testament and Hebrew at Moore Theological College in Sydney, Australia.

11. Andrew G. Shead, "An Old Testament Theology of the Sabbath Year and Jubilee," *Reformed Theological Review* 61, no. 1 (April 1, 2002): 19–20, 22.

12. See Don Blosser, "The Sabbath Year Cycle in Josephus," *Hebrew Union College Annual* 52 (January 1, 1981): 131. See also Robert Grady North, "Maccabean Sabbath Years," *Biblica* 34, no. 4 (January 1, 1953): 506.

13. For an insightful read on the nature of self, see chapter 5, "Autocracy Verses Integrity," in Edwin H. Friedman, *A Failure of Nerve: Leadership in the Age of the Quick Fix*, new ed. (New York: Church Publishing, 2007), 152ff.

Chapter 5: God's Issue with Clenched Fists

1. See also Jeremiah 34:12–17.
2. North maintains that "there is no peg in any historical document for the actual date of any general Sabbath fallow, and much less for a recurrent cycle" (North, "Maccabean Sabbath Years," 514). Several scholars adamantly disagree, including Don Blosser (Blosser, "The Sabbath Year Cycle," 129–30), August Strobel (Strobel, "Die ausrufung des jobeljahres in der Nazarethpredigt Jesu: Zur apokalyptischen tradition, Lk 4:16–30," BZNW 40 [1972]: 45), and Ben Zion Wacholder, who asserts that there is sufficient evidence for the certainty of Sabbath Year cycles "in Palestine from the post-exilic period to the fifth or sixth Christian century" (Wacholder, "Chronomessianism: the Timing of Messianic Movements and the Calendar of Sabbatical Cycles," *HUCA* 46 [1975]: 203).

Movement Two

1. Edwin H. Friedman, *A Failure of Nerve: Leadership in the Age of the Quick Fix*, new ed. (New York: Church Publishing, 2007), 100.

Chapter 6: The Underestimated Danger of Not Listening

1. See also Jeremiah 44:1–6.
2. Marjorie J. Thompson, *Soul Feast: An Invitation to the Christian Spiritual Life* (Louisville: Westminster John Knox Press, 2005), 48.
3. A breathtaking bridge from the Old Testament Sabbath Year regulations to Jesus' New Testament announcement of *release* is built by Shead, who sees a crescendo in the Sabbath and Jubilee emphases that reaches a peak in Jesus' bold recitation of Isaiah 61. Though an extended quote, Shead's explanation is simply too beautiful to paraphrase: "The pinnacle and culmination of this process, in terms of where the OT witness is heading, is the sermon of Jesus recorded in Luke 4. And the key word of the sermon, a word which, almost on its own, carries the process from Leviticus to Luke is ἄφεσις—which brings us to the Septuagint. . . . Indeed, the long evolution of Leviticus 25 can virtually be equated, in the LXX, with the evolution of the meaning of ἄφεσις. One might almost say that

its original legal-economic, and subsequent political edges have rubbed away, leaving behind the word used now in the NT to mean 'forgiveness.' . . . What has been offered since Luke 4 is forgiveness and restoration to a life of sabbatical blessedness in a new creation. Jesus' miracles of release for the oppressed and sight for the blind were signs of this, but the real sign was the miracle of his resurrection from the dead. It is only here that the Day of Atonement timing of Leviticus 25:10 makes complete sense" (Shead, "Theology of the Sabbath Year," 31, 32–33).

Chapter 7: A Curious Remedy for Idolatry

1. Feel free to use the book's PI as a sample and choose a platform that gives you freedom to edit, erase, and amplify. For years I crafted my PIs on legal pads for the drafts and then wrote out a copy in my journal. Currently I do it all on my computer and then print out a copy to attach to my journal for prayer.

Chapter 8: The Sound of Listening

1. See Matthew 11:15; 13:9, 43; Revelation 3:9.
2. See Mark 4:9, 23; Luke 8:8; 14:35.
3. See Revelation 2:7, 11, 17, 29; 3:6, 13, 22.
4. Steven C. Hawthorne, "The Story of His Glory" (lecture, Austin, TX, 1992).

Chapter 9: Seed #3 and the Enemy's Plan B

1. See Matthew 13:1–23, Mark 4:1–20, and Luke 8:4–15.
2. The "eternal fire prepared for the devil and his angels" spoken of by Jesus in Matthew 25:41ff.
3. See Matthew 13:22 and Mark 4:19.
4. "Your inheritance, the kingdom prepared for you since the creation of the world," spoken of by Jesus in Matthew 25:34ff.

Movement Three

1. A. W. Tozer, *The Knowledge of the Holy* (New York: Harper & Row Publishers, 1961), 1–2.

Chapter 10: The Source of Spiritual Misthink

1. Tozer, *The Knowledge of the Holy*, 3.
2. Ibid., 4.
3. Ibid., 2.
4. Spiros Zodhiates, ed., *Lexical Aids to the Complete Word Study New Testament*, comp. and ed. Spiros Zodhiates, Th.D. (Chattanooga, TN: AMG Publishers, 1991), 1659.

Chapter 11: How to Water Thorns

1. Comment from "Crimson from Clarksville, TN," as quoted in "Honey Locust," *Dave's Garden* (blog), accessed October 26, 2016, http://davesgarden.com/guides/pf/go/38373/#b.
2. Brother Lawrence and Frank Laubach, *Practicing His Presence* (Auburn, ME: Christian Books, 1973), 51.

Movement Four

1. Howard Thurman, *Jesus and the Disinherited* (Boston: Beacon Press, 1996), 18, 39.

Chapter 16: New Rules, New Start

1. A long, long, long time ago, I stumbled on a mini-illustration in the back pages of a journal about a woman who let too many people have access to her house and had to take drastic action to regain authority in her own home. The image was the seed idea for the story in chapter 16. Though decades later, this amplified adaption probably resembles its inspiration only vaguely; however, my tendency to be a wee bit obsessive about citing sources compels me to apologize to the wise thinker who penned the mini-illustration that inspired this story. I tried to find you. If you find me, please let me know!

Chapter 17: Changing the Locks

1. Many "Who am I in Christ?" lists are available. Kyle Miller, a biblical counselor, compiled this list. globalcareresponse.org. Used with permission.

Movement Five

1. Excerpted from "A Prayer of Stability," Gloria Hutchinson, *Six Ways to Pray from Six Great Saints* (Cincinnati: St. Anthony Messenger, 1982), 38.

Chapter 18: Faith as a Duet

1. Oswald Chambers, *My Utmost for His Highest: An Updated Edition in Today's Language*, ed. James Reimann (Grand Rapids, MI: Discovery House, 1992), 12.
2. See Isaiah 7:14 and Matthew 1:23.
3. *Merriam-Webster Learner's Dictionary*, s.v. "with," accessed October 22, 2016, http://www.learnersdictionary.com/definition/with.
4. The first definition is "the point around which a circle or sphere is described." *Merriam-Webster.com*, s.v. "center," https://www.merriam-webster.com/dictionary/center, accessed October 27, 2016.
5. Ibid.
6. John W. Peterson, ed., "In the Garden," in *Great Hymns of the Faith*, 9th ed. (Grand Rapids: Zondervan Publishing House, 1970), hymn 264.

Chapter 19: Our Primary Occupation

1. Brother Lawrence and Frank Laubach, *Practicing His Presence* (Auburn, ME: Christian Books, 1973), 69.

Chapter 20: Invited Home

1. This experiment was inspired by Brother Lawrence, who "resolved to make the love of God the end of all [his] actions" (Lawrence and Laubach, *Practicing His Presence*, 45).
2. Brother Lawrence, *The Practice of the Presence of God* (New Kensington, PA: Whitaker House, 1982), 80–81.

Chapter 21: Inheritance Prayers

1. Eat your greens and read your appendices. (One day I hope my children will stumble on this obscure endnote as adults and smile. I love you three to infinity and beyond.)

2. Graham Cooke, *Crafted Prayer: The Joy of Always Getting Your Prayers Answered*, Being with God (Grand Rapids: Chosen Books, 2004), 83–4.

Movement Six

1. Roger Joseph Green, *Catherine Booth: A Biography of the Cofounder of The Salvation Army* (Grand Rapids: Baker Books, 1996), 214–15. Used by permission.

Chapter 22: The Word

1. Tricia McCary Rhodes, *The Wired Soul: Finding Spiritual Balance in a Hyperconnected Age* (Colorado Springs: NavPress, 2016), 65.
2. See www.biblestudytools.com and www.biblehub.com.

Chapter 24: To God About God's Word

1. Robert Jamieson, A. R. Fausset, and David Brown, *Commentary Critical and Explanatory on the Whole Bible* (Oak Harbor, WA: Logos Research Systems, 1997), s.v. Psalm 119:1–176.
2. For a convincing argument of David's authorship, see Rabbi Joshua Maroof's Torah Blog commentary at http://vesomsechel.blogspot.com/2006/11/who-wrote-psalm-119.html.
3. See Hebrews 4:12–13.
4. See Psalm 119:8, 56, 57, 60, 67, 100, 101, 129, 145, 167, 168.
5. See Psalm 119:47, 48, 97, 113, 119, 127, 140, 159, 163, 167.
6. See Psalm 119:15, 23, 48, 78, 97, 99, 148.
7. See Psalm 119:61, 83, 93, 109, 141, 176.
8. See Psalm 119:16, 24, 47, 70, 77.
9. See Psalm 119:22, 31, 55, 69, 146.
10. See Psalm 119:43, 74, 81, 114, 147.
11. See Psalm 119:20, 40, 131.
12. See Psalm 119:51, 82, 157.
13. See Psalm 119:33, 112.
14. See Psalm 119:45, 94.
15. See Psalm 119:102, 110.
16. See Psalm 119:106, 166.

17. Jeanne-Marie Bouvier de la Motte-Guyon, *A Short and Easy Method of Prayer: Praying the Heart of the Father* (Shippensburg, PA: Destiny Image Publishers, 2011), 7.

Chapter 25: When the Word Is Heard and Heeded

1. This section is excerpted from Alicia Britt Chole, *Finding an Unseen God: Reflections of a Former Atheist* (Minneapolis: Bethany House, 2009), 29–30.
2. See Psalm 119:75, 92, 143, 161.
3. See Psalm 119:50, 93.
4. See Psalm 119:104, 128.
5. David McCasland, *Oswald Chambers: Abandoned to God, the Life Story of the Author of* My Utmost for His Highest (Nashville: Discovery House, 1993), 105.

Chapter 26: A Request for More

1. See Psalm 119:25, 28, 37, 107, 116, 149, 154, 156.

Movement Seven

1. C. S. Lewis, *The Screwtape Letters: With Screwtape Proposes a Toast* (San Francisco: HarperSanFrancisco, 2001), 63–64.

Chapter 27: Sploshy

1. If you are wondering why I am speaking about the soul instead of the spirit, it is because I appreciate how the Hebrew word translated *soul* in the OT (נֶפֶשׁ nephesh) and the Greek word translated *soul* in the NT (ψυχή psuchē) are translated elsewhere as "life," "person," "heart," "mind," "body," and "appetite." The mystery of the soul presses us to think about intimacy with God as integrated beings as opposed to processing nearness with God in only a cognitive, emotional, or physical domain.
2. Thoughts from these reflections frame another book I wrote that you may enjoy called *Anonymous: Jesus' Hidden Years . . . and Yours* (Nashville: Thomas Nelson, 2011).

Chapter 29: Our Original Artist

1. This friend is Shannon Bacon. You can find out more about her by visitng her website at http://www.randybacon.com/shannon.

2. The meaning of names can be a slippery certainty, but *Esther* in Persian seems to mean "star" and *Adanna* is Nigerian for "her father's daughter."

Chapter 31: The Positive Power of Pure Pleasure

1. *Chariots of Fire*, directed by Hugh Hudson (Burbank, CA: Warner Brothers, 1981), DVD.

2. See Julian Wilson, *Complete Surrender: A Biography of Eric Liddell, Olympic Gold Medallist and Missionary*, rev. ed. (Milton Keynes, UK: Authentic Media, 2012); Catherine M. Swift, *Eric Liddell (Men of Faith)* (Minneapolis: Bethany House Publishers, 1990); Janet Benge and Geoff Benge, *Eric Liddell: Something Greater Than Gold (Christian Heroes, Then and Now)* (Seattle: YWAM Pub., 1998).

Movement Eight

1. David McCasland, *Oswald Chambers: Abandoned to God, the Life Story of the Author of* My Utmost for His Highest (Nashville: Discovery House, 1993), 205, 259.

Chapter 32: Can ≠ Should

1. Henry D. Thoreau, *Walden and Other Writings*, reprint ed. (New York: The Modern Library, 1950), 290.

2. *Merriam-Webster.com*, s.v. "fast," accessed January 25, 2017, https://www.merriam-webster.com/dictionary/fast.

3. Mike Bickle, *The Rewards of Fasting: Experiencing the Power and Affections of God* (Kansas City, MO: Forerunner Books, 2005), 41.

Chapter 34: Mental Waiting

1. This description is from Frank Laubach. Brother Lawrence and Frank Laubach, *Practicing His Presence* (Auburn, ME: Christian Books, 1973), 10.

Movement Nine

1. Abraham Joshua Heschel, *The Sabbath: Its Meaning for Modern Man* (New York: Farrar, Straus and Giroux, 2005), 6.

Chapter 39: Margin

1. Richard Swenson, *Margin: Restoring Emotional, Physical, Financial, and Time Reserves to Overloaded Lives* (Colorado Springs: NavPress, 2004).

Movement Ten

1. Alicia Britt Chole, *Anonymous: Jesus' Hidden Years . . . and Yours* (Nashville: Thomas Nelson, 2011), 3.

Chapter 42: An Ancient Angst

1. Jeanne-Marie Bouvier de La Motte-Guyon, *Jeanne Guyon: An Autobiography* (New Kensington, PA: Whitaker House, 1997), 238.
2. C. S. Lewis, *The Screwtape Letters: With Screwtape Proposes a Toast* (San Francisco: HarperSanFrancisco, 2001), 40.

Chapter 43: The Silence of God

1. I am unable to find which writing this quote appears in even though the phrase seems unquestionably attributed to John of the Cross. "Silence is God's First Language," Belief.net, http://www.beliefnet.com/faiths/faith-tools/meditation/2004/11/silence-is-gods-first-language.aspx, accessed October 25, 2016.

Movement Eleven

1. Adele Ahlberg Calhoun, *Spiritual Disciplines Handbook: Practices That Transform Us* (Downers Grove, IL: InterVarsity Press, 2005), 41–42.

Chapter 45: The Work of Rest

1. Shane Claiborne, Jonathan Wilson-Hartgrove, and Enuma Okoro, *Common Prayer: A Liturgy for Ordinary Radicals* (Grand Rapids: Zondervan, 2010), 554.

Chapter 46: Come Away

1. Henri J. M. Nouwen, *Making All Things New: An Invitation to the Spiritual Life* (San Francisco: HarperCollins Publishers, 1981), 71.

2. Much of what is covered in these three chapters is excerpted from a small, interactive booklet I wrote called *Ready, Set, Rest Vol. 1: The Practice of Prayer Retreating*. This booklet is available as a free download on my website at www.aliciabrittchole.com.

Chapter 47: Packing Light

1. Some of my favorites are Brother Lawrence and Frank Laubach, *Practicing His Presence* (Auburn, ME: Christian Books, 1973); Richard J. Foster and James Bryan Smith, *Devotional Classics: A Renovaré Resource for Spiritual Renewal* (San Francisco: HarperSanFrancisco, 1990); and Henri J. M. Nouwen, *In the Name of Jesus* (New York: St. Paul Press, 1999).

2. Obvious exceptions would be a laptop if it doubles as your journal and your phone for emergencies.

3. Some have asked if they should bring their favorite movie. I really enjoy a good movie, but since there is a difference between resting and escaping, when I am preparing for a retreat, I ask myself, "Can I truly talk with God and listen for His voice while doing _____?" If the answer is no, I leave it at home.

Chapter 48: Retreat Rhythms

1. www.rrbranson.com.

2. Basilea Schlink, *My All for Him* (Minneapolis: Bethany House Publishers, 2001), 16.

Movement Twelve

1. Henri J. M. Nouwen, *The Genesee Diary: Report from a Trappist Monastery* (Garden City, NY: Image Books, 1981), 85. Excerpt(s) from THE GENESEE DIARY: REPORT FROM A TRAPPIST MONASTERY by Henri Nouwen, copyright © 1976 by Henri J. M. Nouwen. Copyright renewed © 2004 by Sue Mosteller, CSJ, executrix of the Estate of Henri J. M. Nouwen. Used by permission

of Doubleday, an imprint of the Knopf Doubleday Publishing Group, a division of Penguin Random House LLC. All rights reserved.

2. Ibid., 144–45.

Chapter 49: The Overflow

1. Howard Thurman, *Jesus and the Disinherited* (Boston: Beacon Press, 1996), 96.

Chapter 50: Open Eyes

1. "Prayer of Saint Teresa of Avila (1515–1582)," CatholiCity.com, accessed January 26, 2017, http://www.catholicity.com/prayer/prayer-of-saint-teresa-of-avila.html.

Chapter 52: Anticipation

1. *Sayings of Light and Love*, no. 57 as quoted in Richard P. Hardy, *Search for Nothing: The Life of John of the Cross* (New York: Crossroad, 1982), 140.

2. Brother Lawrence and Frank Laubach, *Practicing His Presence* (Auburn, ME: Christian Books, 1973), 6.

ABOUT THE AUTHOR

In person and in print, Dr. Alicia Britt Chole's words perform grace-filled surgeries. Her voice is soothing, her manner is calm, and her messages are piercing. She has often been compared to a sword wrapped in velvet.

An intriguing wordsmith, skillful mentor, and award-winning writer, Alicia speaks internationally and has authored several books including *Anonymous: Jesus' Hidden Years . . . and Yours* and *40 Days of Decrease: A Different Kind of Hunger. A Different Kind of Fast.* Men and women, learners and leaders, across ethnically diverse groups agree: in a culture obsessed with all things new, Alicia brings ancient truth to life.

Alicia holds a DMin in leadership and spiritual formation from George Fox Seminary and serves as the founding director of Leadership Investment Intensives (www.leadershipii.com), a non-profit devoted to providing customized soul-care for leaders in business and ministry.

Alicia lives in the Ozarks of Missouri with her husband, Dr. Barry Jay Chole, their three amazing children (all Choles through the miracle of adoption), two somewhat-less-than-amazing dogs, four truly strange cats, one curiously social guinea pig, and four confused chickens.

Among her favorite things are thunderstorms, jalapenos, wild woods, and pianos in empty rooms. To connect with Alicia, visit www.aliciabrittchole.com and @aliciachole.

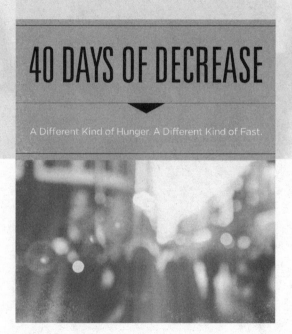

alicia britt chole

40 DAYS OF DECREASE

A Different Kind of Hunger. A Different Kind of Fast.

Thin your life in order to thicken your communion with God through Alicia's book *40 Days of Decrease: A Different Kind of Hunger. A Different Kind of Fast*. In this surprising journey, Alicia guides readers in fasting apathy, injustice, revisionism, and more . . . all for the love of God.

ALSO AVAILABLE FROM
ALICIA BRITT CHOLE

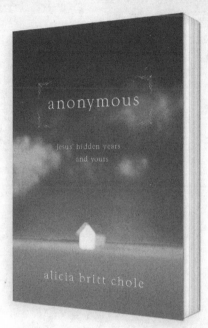

*If you've ever felt unseen and uncelebrated, if it
looks like someone pressed the pause button on your
dreams and potential, this book will breathe fresh
hope and purpose into seemingly barren seasons.*

W PUBLISHING GROUP

AVAILABLE IN PRINT
AND EBOOK